A DREAM AND A PLAN
A Woman's Path to
Leadership in Human Services

A DREAM AND A PLAN

A Woman's Path to Leadership in Human Services

Lorrie Greenhouse Gardella
Karen S. Haynes

NASW PRESS

National Association of Social Workers
Washington, DC

Gary Bailey, MSW, *President*
Elizabeth J. Clark, PhD, ACSW, MPH, *Executive Director*

Cheryl Y. Bradley, *Publisher*
Paula L. Delo, *Executive Editor*
Andre M. Barnett, *Editor*
Gail W. Martin, Editorial Associates, *Copy Editor*
Christina Bromley, *Proofreader*

Cover by Eye to Eye Design Studio, Bristow, VA
Interior design and typesetting by Cynthia Stock, Silver Spring, MD
Printed and bound by Victor Graphics, Inc., Baltimore, MD

Library of Congress Cataloging-in-Publication Data

Gardella, Lorrie Greenhouse.
    A dream and a plan : a woman's path to leadership in human services / by Lorrie
    Greenhouse Gardella and Karen S. Haynes.
       p.   cm.
    Includes bibliographic references.
    ISBN 0-87101-359-2 (pbk.)
       1. Women social workers—United States. 2. Women social workers—
    Promotions—United States. 3. Human services—United States—Administration. 4.
    Leadership—United States. 5. Women executives—United States. 6. Career
    development—United States. I. Title: A woman's path to leadership in human services.
    II. Haynes, Karen S. III. Title.

    HV40.46.G37 2003
    361.3'023'73—dc22   2003061767

Printed in the United States of America

For our parents:

Annette and Milton S. Greenhouse
and
Adelaide and Edward Czarnecki

Contents

Foreword

How many times have you, as a female member of a helping profession, watched a confident, articulate, and seemingly well-put-together woman and wondered whether you and she had anything in common? Have you asked yourself, "How did she become who she is?" Did you ever wish that you could have one hour alone with her, just to talk and ask her questions? Just as Lorrie Greenhouse Gardella and Karen S. Haynes wondered, you would probably ask, "How did you get there? What did you expect? What barriers did you face? What choices did you make? Where did you find support? How do you change the world? How are you leading human services?"

Usually, busy women are so involved in supporting and encouraging others that they do not take the time to identify their own interests and assess their own strengths and weaknesses. Sometimes, as women, we are afraid to look into the mirror and really see ourselves as readily as we look into the faces of others. Women in human services have every right to care about themselves as much as they care about others. We have a right to develop our own careers just as we help others to gain the confidence to develop theirs.

A Dream and a Plan is not simply a book. It is an experience that all of us can share. It is about dreams and disappointments, role models and demons, being turned away and then creating and taking advantage of opportunities. It is about race, class, culture, sexual orientation, and gender. It is about the joy of being part of the community of women and the challenges of surviving and thriving within the larger community.

We do not need to be afraid to look into the mirror. If we look closely, we will see the reflections of countless other women who know our innermost hopes and fears, who share in our triumphs, and who stood where we now stand—striving and determined to reach back and support those whose faces will appear next in the mirror.

Read our stories, learn our lessons, and then, reach back to our sisters.

Ruth W. Mayden, MSW
Director, Program for Families with Young Children
The Annie E. Casey Foundation

Preface

Who We Are and
Why We Wrote This Book

By Lorrie Greenhouse Gardella

When I went to college, I felt that I was walking off the edge of the earth. I had known neighbors who had left for college, but they never seemed to come back! Arriving on campus filled with gratitude and doubt, I found professors who seemed born to their positions. Nearly all of my professors were men, and I remember them lecturing with seamless eloquence in their tweed coats, knit ties, and shiny brown shoes. Although I have been teaching college for nearly 20 years, in my mind's eye, I do not look anything like a professor.

After I graduated from college, I became a social worker. I had often volunteered at social work agencies, and I went to law school and social work school in hopes of combining the two fields. At each phase of my career—consulting in children's law, practicing social work, and teaching social work—people seemed surprised to see me. I was one of only a few women in my law school class and the only white faculty member at a predominantly black college. Today, although I am Jewish, I teach at a Catholic college for women. Entering relationships across racial,

ethnic, and religious divides, I have felt honored by words of acceptance from colleagues, clients, and students: "You are an honorary Latina." "You are an adjunct Sister of Mercy." These are
the imaginary certificates on my office wall. Despite overwhelming evidence to the contrary, I try to be optimistic about race relations, peace, and the possibility of ending hatred, prejudice, and
discrimination. As a social work educator, I try to open opportunities for students while removing discriminatory barriers.

Just as I have never fit my image of a professor, so my students question their place in college. Whether they are young
adults or grandparents, they usually are the first in their families
to go to college. Whether they have lived all their lives in the
same neighborhoods or immigrated across thousands of miles,
they struggle to find time to study while caring for families and
holding jobs. Nearly all succeed, graduating with bachelor's degrees in social work, beginning professional careers, and going
on to earn master's degrees in social work and related fields.
They attribute their success in college to relationships with people
who believe in their abilities, respect their values, and encourage
them to say their dreams out loud.

When my students first decide to become social workers, they
rarely intend to become leaders. Usually, they look forward to
providing direct services to children, families, or communities.
Soon, however, they run up against obstacles to serving their
clients well, obstacles that sometimes arise from the policies and
procedures of human services agencies. As students learn to analyze policies and the possibilities for change, we faculty members encourage them to consider their professional roles more
broadly. How can they effect organizational change from their
current positions in human services? How can they effect change
as leaders? Ultimately, many graduates assume leadership positions in human services organizations.

A *Dream and a Plan* is for women in human services who,
like so many of my students, have yet to discover their potential
for leadership or the professional opportunities before them. They
may be women who entered human services to "give something
back" to their communities but who never considered becoming

leaders of human services organizations. They may be women in paraprofessional positions who are beginning their careers; women in community college, college, or graduate school who are advancing their education; or women in social work, long since graduated from college, who are questioning the distance between the promise and the practice of their profession. With this book, we hope to encourage women in human services to pursue leadership careers.

A Dream and a Plan is also for women and men in human services who already hold leadership positions. Researchers consistently find that women, particularly women of color, rarely find mentors to guide their professional advancement. A second purpose of this book, therefore, is to support current leaders and educators in human services as they mentor women leaders of the future.

Few books encourage women in human services to become leaders. Autobiographies and biographies of women leaders in social work and related fields affirm my students' values, but offer little practical guidance for their careers.[1] Management literature provides more information than inspiration for women with social work values and goals. Most research on women leaders has taken place in large corporations, where, in contrast to women in human services, nearly all the managers are affluent and white.[2] Written from a corporate perspective, these books on women's leadership hold slim hope for changing prejudice and discrimination related to race, ethnicity, sex, sexual orientation, disability, or age. Popular self-help books advise women to deal with sexual discrimination by fitting into the mainstream, transforming themselves rather than transforming their organizations.[3]

Books on women leaders of color in corporations come to the discouraging conclusion that women managers from different racial and ethnic groups do not join together in fighting racial and sexual discrimination.[4] Literature on diversity management takes a more upbeat approach, proposing strategies to end discriminatory practices. Until recently, however, researchers rarely have dealt with more than one type of discrimination at a time. Studies of sexual discrimination have focused on the experiences of white women managers, while studies of racial and ethnic discrimination have focused on the experiences of men.[5]

Although corporate managers and human services managers perform many similar tasks, books by and for women corporate leaders do not address the particular challenges of leading human services organizations. Many women who advance into leadership positions must resist prejudice and discrimination in their careers, but from a social work perspective, women leaders in human services have the greater responsibility "to strive to end discrimination, oppression, poverty, and other forms of social injustice," which is the professional mission of social work.[6]

According to *The Social Work Dictionary*, human services organizations address social needs related to health, education, housing, income, justice, and public safety.[7] In addition, human services organizations promote community and social development, economic development, and civil and human rights.[8] Public agencies, private nonprofit organizations, churches or faith-based organizations, and voluntary associations have historically provided human services in the United States.[9] The government has supported human services organizations directly, by giving them tax dollars, or indirectly, by granting them tax-exempt status. As a result, corporations and human services organizations have distinct missions. While corporations have an obligation to benefit their shareholders or owners, human services organizations have an obligation to benefit the public.[10]

In today's economy, the differences between corporations and human services organizations are becoming less distinct. Public agencies subcontract with private corporations to manage public schools, hospital emergency rooms, and child welfare services. Nonprofit organizations, responding to cutbacks in government funds and faltering private donations, struggle to meet the bottom line. Assuming a corporate management style, some human services organizations recruit their managers from the business world.

In this political and economic context, human services organizations need social workers more than ever in senior leadership positions because social workers have the ethical obligation to advocate with and on behalf of the clients and communities that they serve. As explained by the National Association of Social Workers:

> Social work is the appropriate profession to take a leadership role not only in disseminating knowledge about diverse client groups, but also in actively advocating for fair and equitable treatment of all clients served. This role should extend within and outside the profession.[11]

If social workers are to respond to this challenge, then we need a different kind of management literature, a welcoming literature that introduces the knowledge, skills, and values of leadership as a part of social work practice. Years ago, I found such a book in *Women Managers in Human Services* by Karen S. Haynes.[12] I used the book, to the delight of students, until it went out of print, and I never found anything to replace it. Then I met Karen Haynes when we served together on the board of a national professional association. I asked her whether she would be interested in writing another book on women leaders. So began our collaboration.

For our new book, we decided to bring women leaders from different racial, ethnic, and social backgrounds into focus groups where they would discuss their professional paths, including the obstacles they faced, the resources they used, and the lessons they learned along the way. We imagined the focus groups as a community of mentors who would inspire, inform, and guide readers toward leadership careers. In addition, the focus groups would, by their example, encourage readers to cultivate their own mentoring communities, pursuing professional advancement while also mentoring future generations of women leaders.

In composing the focus groups, we invited a diverse sample of women leaders so that readers from various cultural and social backgrounds would identify with the focus group discussions. Personal and professional networks and national professional associations helped us identify women leaders from various parts of the United States and from various backgrounds in terms of race, ethnicity, national origin, socioeconomic status, sexual orientation, disability, and age.[13] In the end, we held three focus groups that included a total of 23 participating women leaders. Two of the focus groups met face-to-face, and, in a new experience for us, one of the groups met online, a format that allowed us to expand the racial, ethnic, and geographic diversity of participating women leaders.[14]

The women in our focus groups had varied experiences as leaders. All had held leadership positions in human services during their careers, but many of the women also had led other types of nonprofit organizations. As members of our professional associations, a disproportionate number of the women were leaders in social work education or higher education at the time we met them. All the women had advanced educational credentials, most in social work and some in other fields.[15]

In describing their careers, women in the three focus groups identified the greatest barriers to their professional advancement as racial and sexual prejudice and discrimination. Employment discrimination had been and continued to be a major challenge for the women leaders. As we listened to the focus groups, we sharpened the focus of our book.[16] Rather than describing leadership generally or introducing a range of management skills, we would concentrate on women leaders' experiences in resisting discrimination and promoting social change.

In addition to the focus groups, we decided to include Karen in our community of mentors. As a social worker, professor, dean, and university president, Karen had many leadership stories to tell, and equally important, she kept a diary! Karen had been recording her professional experiences since her first administrative position, and the diary was now three volumes long. After we conducted the focus groups, analyzed the transcripts, and identified themes from the focus group discussions, Karen culled her diaries for relevant stories. I then interviewed Karen over several days, taping an oral narrative history of her experiences. Karen's stories complemented stories from the focus group discussions, adding depth to breadth. While we had promised anonymity to the focus groups, Karen spoke on the record.

During the course of our collaboration, I accepted primary responsibility for research and writing. My biggest challenge was to organize all the materials: stories from the three focus groups and from Karen's oral narrative, written excerpts from Karen's diary, and notes from an ever-widening review of the professional literature. With women's stories as the starting place, the book divided naturally into two parts, "Women's Paths to Leadership," which is based on the focus group discussions, and "Leading from an Inclusive Perspective," which presents a vision for leading social change.

The chapters in Part I, "Paths to Leadership," respond to the questions we asked the focus groups. After an overview of the book's purpose (chapter 1), they address questions related to the women leaders' expectations (chapter 2), barriers (chapter 3), choices (chapter 4), and sources of support (chapter 5). Chapters 2 to 5 open with stories from the focus group discussions, as told in the women's own words. The stories are grouped in relation to common themes that arose in the focus group discussions. Themes included experiences or ideas that were shared by the three focus groups or by most women of the same ethnicity. Although I tried to minimize repetition, quotations from the focus groups appear more than once when they relate to more than one theme. Short quotations, such as subtitles to the chapters, are presented in fuller context elsewhere in the book. The women's stories are followed by reflections on "What We Learned," which introduce some theory and research from social work, management, women's studies, ethnic studies, and other fields.[17]

Part II, "Leading from an Inclusive Perspective," explores the potential of women leaders to promote diversity and equity in human services organizations. Chapter 6 offers a conceptual framework for understanding and resisting prejudice and discrimination in organizations, while chapter 7 presents case examples of leadership from Karen's experience. Beyond chapter 7,

Karen's stories are interspersed throughout the book under the heading, "Notes from Karen's Diary." A postscript reflects on our focus group research, including limitations and implications for social work education.

Women leaders in our focus groups had similar perspectives on their careers to women leaders surveyed by Wellesley College researcher Sumru Erkut.[18] In studying a multicultural sample of 60 women leaders in various professions, Erkut found that the women leaders had been tenacious and optimistic throughout their lives. Like women in our focus groups, most women in Erkut's study had enjoyed support from family or community when they were children. On reaching leadership positions, they were as concerned with the growth and well-being of staff as they were with the productivity of their organizations.

However, women in our focus groups told stories unlike any I had found in books about women leaders in corporations. Many authors, for example, assume that families are burdens for professional women.[19] Although women in our focus groups struggled to fill multiple roles in families, in communities, and in human services organizations, they perceived their families as professional assets, as sources of knowledge, skills, and values that guided them in their careers. Working as "outsiders-within,"[20] as the first women or the first women from their racial or ethnic groups to lead their organizations, they did not feel lonely, thanks in part to their families and to extensive networks of support.

Some organizational researchers contrast white women and women of color in corporate management, finding white women more individualistic and less aware of sexual or racial discrimination.[21] In our focus groups, women of various racial and ethnic backgrounds spoke of working for a cause or community beyond themselves. In the context of racially and ethnically heterogeneous focus groups, white women were as likely as women of color to identify employment discrimination in human services.

To my surprise, nearly all the women in our focus groups said that they are successful and happy, and I realized how rarely I have heard women talk about themselves in this way. Literary critics, historians, and linguists find that women tend to understate their accomplishments. Whether in biographies, autobiographies, or everyday conversation, social and literary conventions affect the ways that women tell their life stories and the ways that they are heard. As a result, we are more likely to believe women who speak modestly about their work than women who speak boldly about their achievements and struggles.[22]

As you enter this book, we invite you to make yourself at home with the women leaders and their familiar and surprising stories. If you are a student, volunteer, social worker, or human services provider, turn to the focus groups for role models and guides. Try the questions and suggestions at the end of each chapter as you find your own educational and professional path. If you are a woman or a man in a leadership position, reach out to prospective women leaders. Believe in their abilities, respect their values, and encourage them to say their dreams out loud. And if you are retired as a woman leader, talk about your accomplishments. Tell us your stories so that we may carry them on as leaders and future leaders in human services.

Acknowledgments

Many people contributed to our dreams and plans. We thank, first of all, the women leaders in our focus groups, whose eloquence, vision, and stories form the heart of this book. Saint Joseph College awarded Lorrie a sabbatical; and we thank W. Clark Hendley and Sister Maureen Reardon for their interest and President Winifred E. Coleman, who advises women "to soar." Southern Connecticut State University extended library privileges, and we are grateful to the director and staff of the Buley Library and to Elbert Siegel, director of the department of social work. Rose Meyer and Lynette Colón of Saint Joseph College and DeeDee Canion and Marion Rocha of the University of Houston–Victoria gave moral and technical assistance, while Claire Winfield facilitated the online focus groups.

Leslie Leighninger and the staff of NASW Press made this book possible, and we thank the colleagues, students, and anonymous reviewers who offered suggestions and bibliographic leads. Lynne M. Healy, professor of social work at the University of

Connecticut, commented on several drafts of the manuscript with insight and unwavering support. We were inspired by the friendship and examples of colleagues George A. Appleby, Sally Alonso Bell, Barbara A. Candales, Jimmy E. Jones, Katherine A. Kendall, Robert G. Madden, Julio Morales, Lirio Negroni-Rodriguez, Judith E. Osborne, Shyamala Raman, José Ricardo-Rivera, Jane McVay Rudd, and Sakinah N. Salahu-Din. Finally, we thank our husbands, Peter Gardella and Jim Mickelson, and our children, William Greenhouse Gardella, Eliot Haynes, Kimberly Haynes, and David Mickelson, for helping us retain a balanced perspective, a sense of humor, and continued optimism about women leaders.

Part I

Paths to Leadership

Chapter 1

❧

How Did You Get There?

"Have a dream and a plan."

WOMEN LEADERS FOCUS GROUP

*"Escúchenos, Listen to Us!" was the name of a confer-
ence for Latino/Latina youths in foster care. Rosa had
lived in four foster homes, and she told her story to the
conference in hopes of helping others. At the age of 17,
Rosa was planning to become a social worker. She
dreamed of financial independence and professional success, but she also intended, based on her experience, to
change the way child welfare services are provided to
children and families. The conference facilitator asked,
"If you could meet the Commissioner of Children's Services, what would you say?"*

*"First, I would say, 'Thank you,'" Rosa replied.
"Then I would ask her, 'How did you get there? How
did you get to be you?'"[1]*

This book is for Rosa and other women in human services—social workers, human services providers, students, volunteers, and clients—who may someday
become leaders of human services organizations, and for the current leaders, women and men, who will guide them. The book

3

presents a community of mentors, women leaders in human services who have responded to Rosa's questions by sharing their life experiences, practice wisdom, and professional advice.

Coming from various racial and ethnic backgrounds and from across the United States, the women leaders met in focus groups, where they explored their professional paths, including the expectations that they had, the barriers that they found, and the relationships that sustained them through their careers. They talked about being the first and often the only women, or women from their racial or ethnic groups, to reach their professional positions, and they reflected on the choices that they had made in light of personal, cultural, and professional values and goals. A Mexican American woman leader explained, "I try to contribute to the development of other women leaders by giving a realistic picture of my journey in human services. I share my mistakes and my challenges in an effort to prepare others for the real world."

We promised to protect the women's anonymity and to present their stories faithfully and in their own words. In return, the women spoke thoughtfully, frankly, and with tremendous hope. They did not speak for all women leaders or as representatives of their racial or ethnic groups but as individuals whose experiences may be interesting or useful to the next generation of women leaders. As a white woman leader advised, "No one can tell you how you should be in the leadership world. Listen to the stories of other women as guides; use what is helpful and discard the rest."

The Women Leaders

We held three focus groups, two groups that met in person and one group that met online. A total of 23 women leaders participated from various regions of the United States and from various backgrounds in terms of race, ethnicity, national origin, socioeconomic status, religion, sexual orientation, and age. They were African American, Chinese American, Mexican American, Puerto Rican, South Asian, and white. They were Northerners,

Southerners, Easterners, Westerners, Midwesterners, and from the Pacific Rim. They were married or in domestic partnerships, single, divorced, parents, nonparents, straight, and lesbian (Table 1-1).

All women in the focus groups had held leadership positions in human services organizations during their careers. They had directed community action programs, public child welfare agencies, child guidance clinics, and programs to prevent violence against women. In addition to human services organizations, many of the women had led other types of nonprofit organizations, such as civil rights organizations, national philanthropies, and professional associations. Some of the women had been

Table 1-1
Women in Focus Groups:
Social and Educational Backgrounds

Racial or Ethnic Identity		Highest Educational Degree	
5	African American	18	Social Work
1	Chinese American		2 MSW
3	Mexican American		16 PhD or DSW and MSW
2	Puerto Rican	5	Other fields
5	South Asian		1 JD
7	White		1 MS
			3 PhD

U.S. Geographic Distribution			
3	Mid-Atlantic/Southeast	**Marital Status**	
6	Midwest	2	Divorced
6	Northeast	16	Married or in domestic
1	Pacific Rim		partnership
7	Southwest	4	Single
		1	Widowed

Parental Status
15 Parents
8 Nonparents

NOTE: Total number of women = 23.

elected to political office, while others had moved from human services agencies to schools of social work, where they became professors or deans. Because we used our professional networks to identify women leaders, many of the women were working in social work education or higher education when we met them (Table 1-2).

According to Mildred Joyner, a national leader in social work education, "Social work leaders must . . . paint a vision for the world that can be embraced by everyone. Research that is finding

Table 1-2

Women in Focus Groups: Leadership Positions

Number in position	Position	Women in Multiple Positions (*)
1	City council member/attorney	*
1	Executive director, private nonprofit social services agency	
5	Founder/director, community social services agency	*
7	Dean, school of social work	*
1	Division director, national professional association	
1	Executive director, national professional association	
1	President, national civil rights organization, city chapter	*
1	President, national professional association	*
1	President, national professional association, state chapter	*
5	Professor of social work	* * * * *
1	Senior vice president, national philanthropy	*
5	University administrator/program director	* *

NOTE: Total number of women = 23. Total number of positions = 30.

realistic solutions to racism, sexism, and classism . . . should be a priority in social work."[2] We agree, and we tried to compose focus groups as diverse as the women entering human services today. In seeking out diverse participants, we used a "snowball" sample. Women leaders that we knew from formal and informal networks and professional associations referred us to other women leaders.

Although the resulting focus groups included women from different racial and ethnic backgrounds, they did not include women from all possible demographic groups. We regret, for example, that none of the women whom we invited from First Nations were able to take part. Limitations in diversity are limitations of our research.[3]

So where are the men? Why did we limit our focus groups to women? We chose to focus on the experiences of women leaders because sexual discrimination continues to prevent many women from reaching their full potential in human services organizations.[4] Women represent nearly 70 percent of all paid employees in human services organizations, and more than 79 percent of social workers in the National Association of Social Workers (NASW) are women. Even so, men hold most of the managerial positions. In comparison to women in human services, men move into management earlier in their careers, are promoted faster, and earn significantly higher salaries at every occupational level.[5]

Margaret Gibelman researches employment issues in social work. In a 1997 study of 75 human services organizations, Gibelman found that most of the 4,596 professional employees were women, but 11 percent of women versus 22 percent of men occupied upper-level managerial positions. Controlling for education, age, and field of practice, Gibelman found that men were likely to earn nearly $5,000 per year more than women. The pattern of unequal pay for equal work pervaded human services organizations throughout the United States, including large and small organizations, public and private, secular and nonsecular. Yet social workers typically do not believe that pay inequities exist in their workplaces.[6]

Employment practices that, by intent or effect, limit workforce diversity prevent human services organizations from meeting the needs of the diverse clients and communities that they serve. In Rosa's experience, the child welfare agency had few bilingual, bicultural human services workers to assist her family of origin, to administer or staff group homes, or to recruit and support foster families in the Puerto Rican community. Employment practices that limit workforce diversity also freeze out talented leaders, perpetuating the cycle of discrimination. As Gibelman points out, "Social workers may be more effective in their efforts to eradicate the conditions and effects of oppression and discrimination if they are first able to deal with these realities within their own profession."[7]

Time and Place

The women in our focus groups entered human services in a particular historical context. The civil rights', women's, and gay rights' movements nurtured their values and goals, while federal legislation and government programs expanded their professional opportunities. The Great Society programs of the Lyndon Baines Johnson administration led to the creation of thousands of new jobs in human services and social welfare administration.[8] Title VII, Equal Employment Opportunity, of the Civil Rights Act of 1964 outlawed employment discrimination on the basis of race, color, religion, sex, or national origin. President Johnson gave teeth to Title VII with an executive order that required employers contracting with the federal government to institute affirmative action or "affirmative proactive measures" to increase equality in their workforce.[9] Meanwhile, the Immigration and Nationality Act of 1965 was a watershed in immigration policy, opening U.S. borders to immigrants from Asia, Latin America, and the Caribbean islands.[10]

As employment opportunities expanded in human services, racially dual systems of higher education persisted in Southern states, restricting access of African American and Latino/Latina students to professional education.[11] Women in our focus groups overcame these educational barriers, as they would overcome barriers of employment discrimination throughout their careers. They joined a growing wave of women in the late 1960s and 1970s who sought entry to professions previously dominated by men, including positions of senior leadership in human services organizations.

During the course of their careers, women in our focus groups have seen improvements in the status of women and people of color in human services organizations. A Puerto Rican woman leader remembered being the only Latina student in college and graduate school. She never had a Latino/Latina professor. When Rosa begins college, she will be more likely to have Latina classmates, but Latina professors may still be hard to find.[12] Women in our focus groups remembered being among the few women social work deans in the United States. Today, nearly half the social work deans are women. In their own university systems, however, they are often the only women deans or women deans of color.[13] In the fight against prejudice and discrimination, women leaders of the future have much to learn from women leaders of the past.

ॐॐॐ

Notes from Karen's Diary: Journey

Once upon a time, many years ago, I was preparing for an important journey. This was to be the most exciting, scary, and challenging voyage of my life. I wanted to take the trip; I had competed for the opportunity; and like any good traveler, I had learned all I could, reading about the culture, learning the language, and, to the extent information was available, studying the norms. What made this excursion so significant and so different from my previous travels was that I would be the first outsider to enter this previously closed society! I had to think about a strategy that would provide me an entry without raising barriers and defenses. I knew I would probably be more noticeable as a blonde in this culture, but there was nothing I could do about that (well, okay, I could have done something about that).

The day finally arrived. I felt prepared. As I approached the sacred room, the voices were discernible, although the words were not. I breathed deeply and entered. An immediate and total silence fell upon the group. All eyes turned to me—with panic in them. The natives didn't know what to say or do. I realized that they had probably not prepared for this meeting anywhere nearly as much as I had.

Thankfully, the leader arrived at that moment, greeted me with the traditional tribal greeting, which I recognized and responded to, and showed me a place to sit. The leader introduced me without fanfare or warmth. The ritual had begun.

I felt disoriented by the environment, so strangely dark and large. As I sat, my feet didn't touch the floor. I tensed and then sighed. I could understand the natives' language enough to make sense of most of it, but their body language and facial expressions seemed at odds with their words. I probably needed to learn more of the nuances of this language. I waited politely for someone to ask me to speak, but after some time I realized that I must bravely jump in. I falteringly started and was immediately interrupted. I shrank back, waited, regained my poise, and began to speak again.

Hardly anyone looked at me. No one acknowledged what I said. The discussion continued. I glanced furtively around the chamber. No one else seemed to notice what had happened. Was my diction poor? Had I inadvertently used the wrong tense? Was my accent incorrect or my dress inappropriate? Confused and amazed, I sat back to listen harder, to watch more carefully.

Perhaps it was that I had tried to make eye contact (clearly culturally incorrect) or that I had smiled (this was a serious ritual after all). Perhaps my voice was too soft; the blond hair, too distracting. I gulped and tried again, speaking more loudly, with a serious expression on my face and carefully looking above their heads.

There was no response.

Stunned and stymied, I withdrew, feeling defeated and overwhelmed. "Who could I even ask for help?" I wondered. Lost in thought, I missed the cue. Everyone stood up. The ritual was over. I was thankful, but also concerned. If I did not learn the secrets, I would endure this same confusion over and over. Would I find the answer? Would anyone reach out?

As I was musing on these questions, one of the natives spoke to me in a language I understood! "Karen, how did you enjoy your first deans' meeting?"

ॐॐॐ

Summing Up Chapter 1

- The primary purpose of this book is to interest women in human services in becoming leaders.
- The secondary purpose is to interest current leaders and educators in human services in mentoring women leaders of the future.
- We invited women leaders to participate in focus groups, where they discussed their professional paths, including their values and goals, the barriers they faced, and the relationships that sustained them through their careers.

- Twenty-three women from various racial and ethnic backgrounds and various regions of the United States met in three focus groups.
- All the women had served as leaders in human services, but many had also led other types of nonprofit organizations.
- Coauthor Karen Haynes, a social worker and university president, culled her diary for leadership stories that relate to the focus group discussions.
- Women leaders in the focus groups agreed that sexual, racial, and ethnic discrimination persists in human services organizations.
- According to the focus groups, leading human services involves resisting prejudice and discrimination and promoting social change.

౨ౕ౨ౕ౨ౕ

Action Steps

What do you think, and what can you do about it? If you are finding your own path to leadership in human services, the questions and activities at the end of each chapter will help you explore your potential for leadership, including your values and goals, skills and strengths, and sources of support. Try the questions on your own or in classes, groups, or online discussions. You also may enjoy sharing them with mentors or peer mentors—colleagues, classmates, or friends who are at similar phases in their careers. However, if you are a current leader in human services who is becoming a mentor, try the questions and activities with your mentees—individuals or groups of future women leaders. Each question will lead to many more.

What Do You Think?

What are your hopes and dreams for your future? Identify some dreams that you have had at different times in your life—childhood, adolescence, important transitions in adulthood. How are your dreams changing, and how are they constant? How far into the future do they go?

What Can You Do?

Identify a woman leader who may be a role model for you in the future or, alternatively, who has been a role model for you in the past. Invite your role model to lunch. Ask about her career path, accomplishments, and future goals, and thank her for her example.

Where Can You Read More about Women Leaders in Human Services?

Billups, James O. (Ed.). (2002). *Faithful angels: Portraits of international social work notables*. Washington, DC: NASW Press.

Pantoja, Antonia. (2002). *Memoir of a visionary: Antonia Pantoja*. Houston: Arte Público Press.

Chapter 2

❧

What Did You Expect?

*"I had no expectations
other than to change the world."*

WOMEN LEADERS FOCUS GROUP

Women in our focus groups began their careers with a clear sense of purpose and a vague professional plan. They hoped to achieve financial independence while also making a positive difference for others. They were often "firsts," the first in their families to go to college, the first to live in the United States, the first women or the first from their racial or ethnic backgrounds to reach their professional positions. In the words of a Mexican American woman leader, "My whole life has been filled with having been the first here or there, and this was normal for me."

They did not plan to become leaders. "Leadership is not something we expect," an African American woman leader explained, but in realizing their goals of making a difference and helping their communities, they became agents of change, assuming formal and informal responsibilities for leadership in human services organizations.

The Women's Stories

Family Support

Most women in our focus groups grew up in families that believed in their abilities. Their mothers, in particular, encouraged
them to follow their dreams. As a Mexican American woman
leader told us, "My mother had a beautiful way of instilling this
sense of belief in me and in anything that I undertook in life."
An African American woman leader agreed: "Although my
mother died young, she was a wonderful role model for me and
taught me an awful lot before that happened." Another Mexican American woman leader added, "It was my mother from
whom I drew my inspiration. She had little education, but made
every effort to support my efforts and achievements. She was
always there. She was my best friend."

Growing up in privileged families in India, South Asian women
leaders looked up to family role models, including their fathers
and family friends. For one South Asian woman leader:

> *Achievement was a goal that my mother sponsored in*
> *her children, and there were a lot of heroes close to*
> *home. My father had five illustrious sisters who lived*
> *productive lives that excelled. My mother always held*
> *up these five heroines in front of us as being people*
> *that we should emulate. My grandmother was one of*
> *the first social workers in India to do social work out*
> *of her home, and that was an important aim for me to*
> *follow.*

The women leaders entered social work or human services to
"make a difference," to promote "social justice," and to help
their communities. A white woman leader hoped to improve
social services: "Seeing how the poor were treated when going
to social service agencies, I wanted to be part of whatever would
create some change and make a difference in the lives of people."
A Puerto Rican woman leader hoped to change social conditions:

"I pursued areas of work that were consistent with what I wanted to do, and that was really helping community, moving a community into positions where they could change the social conditions of their lives." Another white woman leader wanted to work for civil rights:

> I graduated from college in 1965 with a BA in government and a mission of social justice. I answered an ad for social workers in Orange County, California. I thought social workers did positive things for civil rights. I got the job, and two years later I went to an MSW program. I had no expectations other than to change the world. My social justice mission was fueled by my mother's stories of my Irish grandfather being turned down for employment because he was Irish and by my parents' belief that social inequality was wrong. They were working class and knew little about college.

The women leaders' families did not always understand their work, but they took pride in their accomplishments. As an African American woman remembered, "My parents defined success by happiness and fulfillment and not necessarily by monetary success. Although they never really understood what a social worker did, they provided support in my endeavors to study social work."

A Puerto Rican woman leader recalled:

> I grew up without a father, and my mother always knew and felt that education was extremely important. When I would bring home good grades she was wonderfully supportive. She never understood what social work was. She'd always ask, "Well, what do you do?" But she knew that it was a successful job.

"That's my mom," agreed another Puerto Rican woman leader.

Perseverance and Hope

Not all the women in our focus groups enjoyed their families' support. Some families opposed their educational and professional goals. Among women from privileged backgrounds, a Chinese American woman leader, educated in Hong Kong, remembered her family's objections to her studying social work, and several South Asian women leaders noted that social work was not a "preferred profession" in their families. Among women from low-income backgrounds, a Mexican American woman leader overcame her father's opposition to her going to college:

> *I came from a large family of 11 and lived in a poverty-stricken area of Houston. My parents were recent immigrants with no formal education and a rural upbringing. My father thought men were the breadwinners and women were raised to be good wives and mothers, so an education beyond high school was a waste. Educators and administrators felt that I, as a minority woman, could not possibly get admitted into any university. I soon realized that these educators were only functioning with what they had learned and accepted in their own lives. I knew their world was not for me, so I decided to go around them, not to accept things as they were, but to try to change things for myself and for others. If I didn't know something, I could research, I could ask questions, I could act on my own accord. Many times when others saw my tenacity, they lent me a helping hand. I never gave up hope in getting my career going. I realize now that the barriers weren't really barriers, but God's way of preparing me for what lay before me.*

Women in our focus groups pursued their goals with perseverance and hope. All the women achieved college educations and eventually went on to earn advanced degrees in social work, law, or related fields. Many women alternated between working and returning to school. Blocked in one direction, they tried

another, using each experience to learn skills and to build relationships with new communities. As an African American woman
leader said:

> *I always wished that I had been born later. The civil
> rights', equal rights', and voter rights' struggles, coupled
> with economic disadvantages—each inhibited what I
> wanted to do and when I wanted to do it. I wanted to
> go off to undergraduate school but couldn't afford it;
> wanted to go immediately to graduate school, but the
> ones I chose were not open to African Americans;
> wanted to work in Houston for my first job, but mi-
> nority hiring was minimal. Each professional position,
> while a struggle to attain, prepared me for the next.*

Cultural Wisdom

Although they may have had more formal education than their
parents, the women leaders attributed professional accomplishments to lessons they had learned at home. Families were sources
of values, skills, and cultural wisdom that informed their professional lives. A Mexican American woman leader remembered:

> *My grandmother used to say that a person of culture
> was one who could feel at home with rich or poor,
> one that could carry a conversation with whomever
> one was working, one who treated others with respect.
> Basically, I have measured professional success not by
> the yardstick imposed by society, but rather by that
> given me by my culture. I have been able to integrate
> personal, cultural, and professional values and goals
> by not losing sight of where I came from.*

Another Mexican American woman leader recalled:

> *I came from a poor background, and my father's teach-
> ing of the work ethic came in handy. It disciplined my*

*life and made the enormous hours of study possible
and the goal of becoming an attorney attainable. My
parents' strong teachings of honesty and pride in your
name came into play when running for public office.
My cultural background also facilitated my ability to
accept the diversity of others and made it easier for
me to work with people of different backgrounds.*

It was not always easy to meet their families' expectations.
Most families hoped that the women would succeed professionally while also excelling as wives and mothers. An African American woman leader explained:

*As minority women, I'm not sure we are acculturated
to feel we should be leaders. Your family and friends
hope you will be successful and that you will do well.
And if you're a woman, you should do well enough to
get married, but not so well that you won't be mar-
riageable. It's like, no matter how many degrees you
get, an MA, an MSW, if you get another degree, you'll
never get an MRS! So leadership is not something that
we expect. It just may occur as we are competent in
what we do, and other people confer it. Men expect to
be leaders, but it's a different challenge for women.*

Community Service

Beyond their families, women leaders remember finding role
models in their communities, although they did not always find
them in school. A Puerto Rican woman explained, "I was always alone in school. There were no Latino teachers in any of
the schools I went to or in college or graduate school, so I never
had someone to look up to." On the other hand, a Mexican
American woman said:

*My relationships with my first teachers were very im-
portant. Some were good relationships and helpful,
and others were hurtful. The good relationships helped*

*me overcome some of the damage from other teachers
that were critical, prejudiced, or just plain mean. My
teachers were my first true role models. My fourth-
and fifth-grade teachers were Hispanic men. They were
important to me, because it was the first time I knew
that Hispanics could be college graduates.*

Many women in our focus groups entered human services
through community service as adolescents or young adults. As
described by an African American woman leader:

*The community is where you emerged from. In the
African American community, the community organizations, the sororities and the Urban League are often
where women get an opportunity to develop and practice leadership skills. You may find yourself president
of some organization that the black community re-
veres as much as being the associate dean somewhere
else. They're happy for you that you're the president
of the Links [Inc.] or the Deltas [Delta Sigma Theta],
and when you enter the professional arena, you bring
a repertoire with you—maybe unappreciated by others, and maybe not even on your résumé. But you have
learned already about the management of people and
how things go and certainly the racism and the sexism
that are out there. You arrive with a whole background
of leadership skills that no one knows you have.*

The women leaders formed lasting relationships in community organizations. A Puerto Rican woman leader remembered:

*Someone offered me an opportunity to go and work
in the Department of Welfare, something I had never
heard of. There I met some young Puerto Rican women
that were becoming active in the community. That
connection then led me to a whole new way of life,
and from there I went into social work, which was
very natural to what I was invested in.*

Resilience and Risk

Women in our focus groups did not take straight paths to leadership positions. They changed professional directions to widen the social impact of their work or to bypass racial and sexual discrimination. As a Mexican American woman leader explained:

> *I began as a teacher, knowing that teaching was not my ultimate goal. These years greatly influenced my career choice. When I noticed behavioral changes in children, I realized that something was going on at home that was influencing their behavior. I wanted to learn about human behavior and to do something about that.*

Another Mexican American woman leader changed careers when she lost confidence in the criminal justice system:

> *When I first started my career, I already had a family of three, and I needed to begin where I would acquire the most legal experience in the shortest amount of time. I was looking for a position that would help my community, so I became a prosecutor. As a minority, I had seen the horrible consequences of crime from a victim's perspective. It wasn't until I served four years in this position that I realized that I was part of a criminal justice system that was so lopsided. I saw a majority of young minority men being prosecuted. My expectations of this career road were shattered, but a time of introspection launched me into my next career—politics.*

Accepting Ambiguity

Women in our focus groups learned to balance planning for the future with attending to the present. Career plans are useful, they advised us, as long as you are ready to change them. In the words of a white woman leader who was fighting against cancer, "Life doesn't always go the way we plan or want it to go. Goals and plans are a necessity, but we have to be flexible and know when to go with another option, and more importantly, to have another option."

In the shifting professional landscape of human services, women in our focus groups could not always predict the obstacles or opportunities on their paths. A white woman leader valued the unexpected turns in her career:

> Had I decided earlier that I wanted to be an administrator, I probably would have followed a much more direct path and accomplished things a lot sooner. I also might not have had many tremendously interesting and exciting adventures.

A Mexican American woman leader agreed:

> My advice to others is to have a dream and a plan. Be sure to pay attention to your professional environment so that you can take advantage of opportunities that may not have been a part of your specific plan. There have been times in my life that I ended up doing things I had not planned to do, but the opportunity came up and I decided to take advantage of it. The unplanned experience had a positive impact on my professional development as well as contributed to some of the successes I achieved. Had I not been paying attention to something that was not in my plan, I would have missed out on some great opportunities.

Success

As they advanced into leadership positions, the women leaders never gave up on changing the world. As an African American woman leader stated:

Success is—I don't want to say the power, because that's a little heavy—but the opportunity to make a difference and to really do something. Life is different for someone else because I am here. And I consider that success.

A white woman leader agreed: "I define success as having made a positive difference. I have made the world a better place and have not only worked for social justice, but also have served as an example for others to do so."

The women leaders had a holistic view of their careers. A Mexican American woman leader told us, "I define success not just in terms of my career, but my overall life." Looking back on their life's work, many women used the word "integrity" to consider how well they had realized their values, respected relationships, and positively influenced others. Another Mexican American woman leader said, "I would define success as being able to accomplish one's goals in life, helping others to reach theirs, and doing this with grace, dignity, and integrity." An African American woman leader explained:

I am neither rich nor famous. Although many others consider those factors the determinants of success, they are not my measurements of success. I think I am successful because I have been able to accomplish career goals, both planned and unplanned. The work that I have done in a variety of settings has made a positive impact on clients as well as organizations. I have been able to maintain high standards while maintaining my personal and professional integrity. And most important to me, I have always enjoyed my work.

Most women had relational definitions of success. They assessed their work in terms of how well they had met responsibilities to families, communities, professional colleagues, and future generations of leaders. In the words of a South Asian woman leader,

Success for me is balancing my relationships, doing what is necessary for people in different areas of my life—my mother in India, my daughter in another state, my friendships—meeting various people's needs and maintaining my relationships with them to the best of my ability.

An African American woman leader similarly measured personal and professional goals in terms of her relationships with family and community:

I consider myself successful because I wanted to run my own nonprofit organization, and I do. I wanted to experience the joy of marriage and motherhood and succeeded at that. I wanted to live to see my boys grow up to be contributing men to their society without being tainted with problems in the environment such as drugs or crime, and they succeeded. I wanted my parents to live long enough to enjoy the benefits of each of their children's successes, and they did. I wanted to have a life of activity within the community and my church where I could contribute my additional time and support, and I do. So I consider myself to be quite successful.

For some women in our focus groups, spirituality and spiritual relationships contributed to success, as in the reflections of a Mexican American woman leader:

I feel that I am successful. I have found that balancing mind, body, and spirit, I can appreciate life at any given moment. God has given me so much to be grateful for, and knowing this, I can enjoy and be at peace with myself. Life requires for us to live every moment and give it our all.

For a South Asian woman leader, personal, professional, and spiritual relationships were part of a seamless whole:

When I look back and think of success in my own terms, I am successful in that I cherish my wealth of friendships. I cherish the life of the mind. I cherish the great fidelity in marriage. And above all, I cherish the fact that faith and interfaith give me a lot of satisfaction. So is success money? No. Is it prestige? No. But whatever I can do as a spark in the universe, I am doing, and I am happy about it.

What We Learned

Family Values

The women in our focus groups learned cultural knowledge and values from their families. Strengthened by religious faith, they respected traditions from the past while also looking to the future and contributing to cultural change. These experiences are reflected in research on African American, Latina, and South Asian women.[1]

For African American women, families have served as a "refuge against racism," as Jalna Hanmer and Daphne Stratham explain, and African American women are likely to accept their families as sources of stress and support.[2] According to Audre Lorde, African American women have a historical consciousness.[3] As expressed in the motto of the National Association of Colored Women, "Lifting as we climb," African American women are aware that they stand on the shoulders of their ancestors as they, in turn, make sacrifices for the future.[4] Edith Lewis attributes the relational skills of African American women to their family life. In her words, "Women from the African diaspora are recognized worldwide for their skill at developing . . . connections among themselves and others."[5]

True to this research, African American women in our focus groups spoke often of their families. They had family responsibilities whether they were married, single, parents, or nonparents. In their professions as in their families, they were aware of participating in history, and they expressed gratitude to social workers of the past, reverence for elders, and commitment to future generations of women leaders. Like other women in the focus groups, they had relational definitions of success.

Mexican American women and Puerto Rican women in our focus groups had distinct cultural heritages, but they shared a commitment to family. Lorraine Gutiérrez and Zulema Suarez explain that "familism" is a core cultural value for Latinas, whatever their heritage country.[6] Latino families often value traditional gender roles, according to these researchers, but women's roles are changing as Latinas enter higher education and participate in the labor force.[7] Women in our focus groups remembered intergenerational tensions as they pursued educational and professional goals, but they also remembered their families' love, pride, and support.

South Asian women leaders also had strong family values. Many women in our focus groups remembered their mothers as role models, but South Asian women leaders also identified with their fathers as professional examples.[8] Coming from highly educated, professionally oriented families in India, the women were expected to go to college, earn advanced degrees, and excel at homemaking and professional careers.[9] The South Asian women leaders hoped to widen the career choices open to their daughters and to loosen expectations for women's roles at home. Like other women in our focus groups, they were strongly committed to serving their communities and to improving opportunities for women. As global feminists, they sought a balance between cultural tradition and social change.[10]

Leadership and Success

Whatever their race or ethnicity, women in our focus groups learned from their families to hold high standards for their lives and their work. Although they did not always expect to become leaders, they prepared to assume responsibilities for leadership throughout their lives. Their capacities, skills, and values as leaders were based in particular relationships and greater social purpose. The women leaders met challenges with perseverance and hope. They accepted ambiguity and risk while pursuing their visions for the future. These were capacities for social action. They maintained lifelong relationships with family, communities, and organizations, while also reaching out to new communities. As a result, they observed the environment from various points of view. These were skills for social learning. Finally, the women leaders resisted prejudice and discrimination. As they fought against employment discrimination in their own careers, they promoted diversity and equity in human services organizations. These were values for social justice. As a white woman leader explained, "My social justice mission was inspired by my parents, who believed that inequality is wrong" (Figure 2-1).

Figure 2-1
The Making of Women Leaders

I decided not to accept things as they were . . .

*I brought into my place of work my sense
of belonging in a community . . .*

*My whole life has been filled with having been
the first here or there, and this was normal for me . . .*

Social Action Capacities	Social Learning Skills	Social Justice Values
Perseverance and hope	Building relationships	Social identity
Resilience and risk	Relating to diverse communities	Social responsibility
Acceptance of ambiguity	Observing the environment	Integrity
Vision for the future	Adapting to change	Diversity and equity

I planned, I prepared, I persevered, and I prayed all the way.	*Each multicultural relationship made me a more open and accepting person.*	*I always am carrying more than myself.*

Capacities for social action, skills for social learning, and values for social justice prepared the women to lead from an inclusive perspective, a perspective based on social responsibility, participatory decision making, appreciation for diversity, and an expansive understanding of power (Figure 2-2). The women leaders' inclusive perspective on leadership and their holistic understanding of success are consistent with the views of some feminists, social workers, and organizational theorists who have written about how to lead.

Social work researchers Nan Van Den Bergh and Lynn B. Cooper present "feminist visions for social work" as holistic worldviews that eliminate false dichotomies, link the personal and the political, value process equally with product, and reconceptualize power.[11] Women in our focus groups rejected "false dichotomies" between family and work or between personal and professional relationships and goals. They realized the

Figure 2-2
Leading from an Inclusive Perspective

*I wanted to be part of whatever would create some change
and make a difference in the lives of people.*

Social responsibility
I looked for a position where I could help my community.

Participatory decision making
I hardly ever take for granted that my worldviews reflect anyone else's.

Appreciation for diversity
I see how enriching it has been to grow up and live in two worlds.

Expansive understanding of power
I have taken a proactive approach to move other women forward.

concept that "the personal is political" by promoting the social good through particular relationships in families, communities, and their professions. Valuing integrity, they attended to process and product: "My greatest success is in having accomplished the goals I have set and maintaining my integrity at the same time," a Mexican American woman leader explained. Rejecting money and prestige as signs of success, they "reconceptualized power" as having "the opportunity to make a difference and to really do something," in the words of an African American woman leader.

In addition to feminist principles, women in our focus groups expressed social work principles in their understanding of leadership and success. Michael Rank and William Hutchison surveyed national leaders in the social work profession to learn how they perceive leadership.[12] According to the survey, social workers look for such leadership qualities as commitment to social justice and appreciation for human diversity. Social workers prefer an altruistic and participatory leadership style, and they have a systemic perspective on leadership, appreciating that as the head of an organization, a leader has responsibility toward the greater social good. Leaders of human services coalitions agree, according to a study by Terry Mizrahi and Beth Rosenthal.[13] Coalition leaders attribute their success to building trusting relationships, encouraging communication, and including stakeholders in decision making.

Social workers are not alone in their views of good leadership. Researchers come to similar conclusions about leadership when they study corporations in times of change. At the Center for Gender in Organizations, Joyce Fletcher, Roy Jacques, and their colleagues find that effective leaders use a set of interpersonal skills called "relational practice" to nurture relationships, improve communications, and effect cultural change in organizations.[14] Francis Hesselbein, concerned with the challenges of the global economy, recommends that organizational leaders build relationships within organizations and with diverse communities.[15] Drawing from recent discoveries in biology, mathematics, and physics, Margaret Wheatley compares organizations to living systems where "power is the capacity generated by relationships."[16] In *Leadership and the New Science,* she describes effective leaders as those who cultivate relationships, live by their values, share information widely, and welcome participation in decision making.

Like women in our focus groups, Karen looked to relationships and values as the measures of her success.

ॐ ॐ ॐ

Notes from Karen's Diary: Leadership

Early in my career, I would not have understood the difference between management and leadership, between positional authority and the power that comes from modeling values and building relationships. I have come to value "walking the talk." It is easy to talk about a set of values and institutional principles. It is more difficult to examine whether you adhere to them on a daily operational basis.

There are ways to measure whether someone has been a good leader, but I have come to appreciate important elements of leadership that are less quantifiable. For example, a leader should do no harm. You can get things done, but leave personal devastation in your wake. I'd rather get good things done and do good things for people. I work toward improved organizational climate and internal communication, but these goals are difficult to measure. They are not noticed except as they increase external measures, such as funds raised or programs grown.

Leaders have to stop talking and listen, listen to things they don't want to hear. One of the pitfalls in achieving positional authority is that we think we know it all. We don't know it all. There are lots of outsiders who do not talk to us. We need to invite and encourage, or at least not close down and discourage, all kinds of communication.

I have had an incredible amount of power. I've had a lot of people who would work with me, go the extra miles, because they had been included in the vision and felt that they were an empowered part of the organization. I don't use control in the traditional sense. It has no meaning in terms of effectiveness and doing the right thing. Control makes people feel controlled.

I still find myself utilizing old definitions of power that I know don't work. I find myself caught up in them and then feel disempowered. So it is important to keep talking with myself about what power isn't, to be able to move away from concerns about actions or decisions that may not look powerful if they will help build an organization, change a culture, or be more humane.

After several years of being dean of a social work school and building shared governance, I had a call from the university president: Would we take over another program? I was flattered, and I thought this would be good for the school. I didn't say, "Let me go back and talk to people." Rather, I told the faculty and staff at the end of a meeting: "Oh, by the way, we're taking over this program." I got caught up in the power thing; that's how a lot of decisions get made. I didn't want to seem to be asking permission or to seem that I wasn't in control. I jumped the process, and my faculty and staff didn't agree with the decision I had made.

It was a hard weekend getting there, but I called the president and told him that we couldn't do it. In the long term, I don't believe I lost credibility in his eyes. Still, it is hard to be really committed to changing the culture of a university at a table where all the other administrators would say, "Yes, we can go back and do this tomorrow." It is not a group in which process is valued. Action is valued. So authenticity is important to leadership—knowing yourself and your values, personal and professional, knowing which lines you're not willing to cross.

ॐ ॐ ॐ

Women in our focus groups developed their approach to leadership over time. They met barriers of prejudice and discrimination as they advanced into senior leadership positions, but in the face of prejudice, they refined their capacities, skills, and values as leaders and agents of change.

ॐ ॐ ॐ

Summing Up Chapter 2:
Themes from the Focus Groups

- Women leaders entered human services to achieve financial independence, to make a positive difference, and to help their communities.
- Most grew up in families that believed in their abilities.
- Their mothers were important role models.
- Most families supported the women's educational and professional goals, but some families opposed them.
- Families taught values, skills, and cultural wisdom that the women used in their work.
- The women met obstacles with perseverance and hope.
- They changed the directions of their careers while holding onto long-term goals.
- Many women drew strength from religious faith.
- The women leaders understood integrity as fulfilling relationships and living their values.
- They considered themselves successful.

- They defined success as making a positive difference through relating with others, living with integrity, accomplishing goals, and enjoying their work.

⫘⫘⫘

Action Steps

What Do You Think?

How have you made a positive difference in the lives of your family and friends, your community, or your workplace? How have earlier generations opened possibilities for you? How do you hope to be remembered by future generations? How have you improved the lives of other people, even people you may never know?

What Can You Do?

List the values, skills, and personal qualities that help you accomplish your goals. Review your list with someone you trust, and ask her or him to identify any strengths that you overlooked.

Where Can You Read More about Women Leaders' Careers?

Carlton-LaNey, Iris. (Ed.). (2001). *African American leadership: An empowerment tradition in social welfare history.* Washington, DC: NASW Press.

Hartman, Mary S. (Ed.). (1999). *Conversations with powerful women.* New Brunswick, NJ: Rutgers University Press.

Chapter 3

What Barriers Did You Face?

*"There is a difference between being seen as a
curiosity and being seen ... for who I am."*

WOMEN LEADERS FOCUS GROUP

"Have there been any barriers to your professional advancement that haven't come up yet in our conversation?" we asked a focus group. Everyone laughed. An
African American woman replied, "Other than race and sex?
There's more?"

Women leaders in our focus groups faced barriers of racial,
ethnic, sexual, and heterosexist discrimination in their careers.
They worked in the presence of prejudice, and their work—identifying, defending against, getting around, and fighting discrimination—was never done. In the words of a Mexican American
woman leader: "What I worry about is overcoming the barriers
not for myself, but for those who come after me."

The Women's Stories

Coming-of-Age

Racism was a coming-of-age experience in the adolescence of the
African American, Mexican American, and Puerto Rican women

in our focus groups, who learned in high school to recognize racial discrimination without accepting the limitations that it imposed upon them. An African American woman leader recalled:

> *When I was growing up in Baltimore, I went to neighborhood schools that I could walk to, and they were all-black schools. Then I went to an all-girls high school where I was one of a very few students of color. A group of girls from my junior high were considered bright, and we were sent there. Our teachers never told us to watch out, what to look for. They just said, "You can do it." Twenty, thirty years later, we talked about how frightened we were. We didn't know about racism as we began to experience it. When I told my high school counselor that I thought I wanted to work in occupational therapy, she said to me, "There are no jobs like that for colored girls." So I got no guidance about where to apply for college.*

African American women leaders were the only women of color in our focus groups whose parents had been born on the U.S. mainland. Their parents tried to prepare them to survive in a racist world:

> *I was one of a few minorities in my high school in Boston, and in those days, there used to be a very important young political organization called Girls' State. Girls were elected to play out the state government, and if you were elected governor of your state, you went to Washington, DC, to play out Girls' Nation. In my state, I got elected governor. It turned out, however, that Washington was segregated at the time I came along. They would not accept a black girl in the hotel for the proceedings. There was another state that also had elected a black governor, but they decided not to send anybody. My state sent the lieutenant governor, and I was really crushed. My parents never realized how hurt I was. Their attitude was, "You have done*

extraordinarily well to be elected governor, but you're black and you cannot expect to get what everybody else gets. Don't worry about it, and put it behind you."

While some women leaders were learning lessons of racism in U.S. schools, others were resisting sexism as students in India. South Asian women leaders with backgrounds in science arrived in the United States prepared for sexual discrimination in the workplace: "The behavior patterns of male engineers are universal!" They were unprepared for racial and ethnic stereotyping:

I find that there is a way of looking at me. I am a curiosity. There is a difference between being seen as a curiosity and being seen as competent, being seen for who I am. From time to time a few clients will outwardly ask, "Do you think that you can deal with this?" or "What is your background?" When they ask, then you can clarify yourself. When people know something about you, they know who you are and what your belief is; then it puts you just on a human level, one person to another. But colleagues don't ask, and there is that aspect of: "How can you come from this country where there are snakes and tigers and elephants running around and cows walking everywhere? How can you know of something here?" People have very mistaken notions of something very far away and exotic and of you as a product of that place.

Another South Asian woman leader understood her response to racism as a developmental process:

The place where I work uses me as a statistic: "Isn't it wonderful that we have three women of color?" At first, I wondered, "Why do people behave this way towards me? Did I do something wrong?" Then there was a period of anger. And now I watch this with humor. It's a progression, and you are only able to come to terms with it at a certain stage in your life.

Being a Woman

Women in the focus groups could not always tell which prejudice, racism or sexism, was blocking their path. Sometimes prejudices related to sexual orientation, socioeconomic status, religion, or age added to the mix. A Puerto Rican woman leader remembered:

> *In the 1970s, I rose very quickly up the ranks of the antipoverty program. I became the deputy regional director of the biggest region. I was the only woman in a senior management position, a young Latina woman. When the director left, I was made acting director. And I was acting director and acting director, and they kept looking for a man! The national director said in an open room, "I will be damned if I'm going to appoint a woman to my biggest region!" I'd always thought the problem was my race and my ethnicity, but this was when it hit me—being a woman, in some circles, is a huge disadvantage!*

Looking back to the beginnings of their careers, women leaders remembered their early battles against sexism. They had no historical precedents to guide them, no role models or peers to consult. Sometimes the women blamed themselves or other individuals for what they would later understand as systemic discrimination.

ぷぷぷ

Notes from Karen's Diary:
Barriers

At the beginning of my career, there were many barriers that I didn't identify as such. Like many women who are naïve about organizational rules or games, I internalized barriers. I looked to myself as the reason for prejudice, stereotyping, and discrimination.

My first job interviews in 1970 consistently included questions about my marital status, my anticipation of having children, and my husband's expectations for my job. There wasn't yet much advice for women or legislation to help handle these difficult and irrelevant questions. However, by 1973, the women's movement and my own work-related experience had heightened my sensitivity to the structural inequities.

As a full-time faculty member at a large public university, I went into the department chairman's office to inquire about the university's maternity leave. The chairman's response was, "Karen, we'll be so sorry to see you leave."

I was confused. "I just want a few weeks off for maternity leave," I replied.

"We don't have maternity leave. You must resign and take your chances of being rehired."

I was dumbfounded. I went home, thought about it, and returned to his office one or two days later to ask what other women faculty had done. He told me they had resigned. I left to continue to ponder my options. There had been relevant recent federal legislation, but did I want to stir up the waters? I returned to the chairman's office and informed him that I believed this was unfair and in violation of federal law. I wanted to take the issue to the Board of Regents. That would be a mistake, he warned. It was the Board of Regents who determine salary increases and make tenure and promotion decisions. "How will that matter if I'm unemployed?" I countered. It took three separate requests to the Board of Regents to be allowed to take a maternity leave, to use accrued vacation time for maternity leave, and not automatically resign if I needed more time.

The next major setback was years later when I was teaching at a different public university after completing my doctoral degree in 1979. The dean asked me to consider directing the undergraduate social work program. Before accepting the position, I assumed that it would be responsible to look at what I needed to do the job successfully. I returned to the dean's office several days later with a list of some requirements: secretarial support, travel monies, a specific title, and an increase in salary for moving from a 10-month to a 12-month contract and from teaching to administration.

The dean became enraged: "You cannot make the rules and force me to play the game!" He went on to inform me that he would make sure that I never received tenure. The position was offered to a male faculty member who received everything I had asked for.

ॐ ॐ ॐ

It Takes Courage

Like Karen, women in the focus groups were often the first women or the first from their racial or ethnic backgrounds in their professional positions. An African American woman remembered:

> *I was special assistant to the president at a very male-oriented institution, and at the cabinet meetings, I would be the only female present and certainly the only person of color. I had to kind of get used to that environment and find my way through. It takes a lot of courage.*

A white woman leader recalled:

> *Early in my career, I was the only out lesbian or gay person on the faculty and often the only identified feminist. Others would encourage me to speak out in a meeting and then remain silent themselves rather than lending support.*

The sexism in her professional associations surprised another white woman leader:

> When I became a dean at my university, the adminis-
> trators in charge were men. I had anticipated that I
> would experience discrimination but I didn't. They
> made every effort to be inclusive. At the same time, I
> participated in the state association of social work
> deans. They were all men, and I want to tell you, they
> were exclusive. They were not friendly; they were not
> embracing. That was a very hard lesson for me to learn.
> The national deans' meeting was that way as well.
> When I first came in, there were very few women, and
> we bonded together.

As "firsts," the women leaders had a sense of hypervisibility, a feeling that whatever they did would be noticed and judged against stereotypical standards. When they succeeded, they would be seen as exceptions to the stereotype, but when they made mistakes, they would prove the rule. In the words of a Puerto Rican woman leader, "I have always felt alone, or people made me feel alone by saying, 'You're not like other Puerto Ricans; you're an exception.'"

In response to stereotypes, most of the women felt responsible for representing a larger group. As a white woman leader explained,

> I always feel that I am carrying more than myself.
> Maybe because I'm in an institution where all the other
> leaders are men, I'm mindful that I speak for women.
> I'm aware that when I do something, I have to do it
> well. It's not about me, but it's about womankind.

An African American woman leader agreed:

> I certainly feel that how I do things reflects on other
> African Americans in general and on women in particu-
> lar. It is a burden at first, but things are changing a little
> bit and you get a little more support than you used to.

Under the Surface

As the social and political environment changed, and as civil rights legislation was enforced, employers frowned on blatant expressions of prejudice against women or racial and ethnic groups. Explicit discriminatory policies were replaced by implicit practices that hid opportunities from the women's view. A Puerto Rican woman leader explained, "In this day and age, those barriers are hidden under the surface. Sometimes you're not aware of them; they are not in your face, but the opportunity somehow is not there for you." A white woman leader agreed:

> *It was easier to confront prejudice when it was spoken aloud. Now it is like trying to capture fog. Those who would just as soon eliminate feminists, lesbian women, or people of color from their midst have learned to cloak their views so that these attitudes are not easily identified. To confront this continued bias is to risk being labeled paranoid.*

To identify barriers and opportunities in their organizations, the women needed insiders' knowledge and information, but few women in our focus groups had mentors to guide them. In the words of a Puerto Rican woman leader, "I have yearned for role models that are Hispanic or Latina professionals and have been unable to find them."

A South Asian woman leader explained, "It's difficult to find mentors in the working environment, because you don't fit the image of a competent type." Another South Asian woman leader agreed:

> *I had supportive friends when crises developed, but I never had a mentor. It is a lonely place to have those barriers to entry, the lack of access. When you look around, you see that so-and-so went to lunch with so-and-so and that led to another job, and you don't get to that kind of entry.*

Different Standards

As far as the women could tell, their work seemed to be evaluated differently from the work of white men. A Mexican American woman leader noted, "There is a different set of criteria applied to women of color; yet, one is never quite sure what the criteria are." As a white woman leader who is a university professor observed:

> I realized quite late that mentoring and job assignments in my school varied, depending on race, gender, and sexual orientation. The white straight guys were encouraged to do activities directly tied to promotion and tenure, while the rest of us did all the maintenance duties of the school. We expected to be equally rewarded, but this hasn't happened. Many of us have tried to explain this phenomenon to the senior faculty, all straight white guys, and they just don't get it. When one is accustomed to privilege, equality feels like discrimination.

The women leaders tried to break the codes to organizational policies and practices and to decipher organizational criteria for assigning tasks, evaluating work, and rewarding accomplishments. In response to subjective criteria, they tried for perfection. A Chinese American immigrant woman leader, compensating for "slightly accented English," never spoke in meetings without a written text. "I work doubly hard at any task because of the amount of time I put in for preparation: writing the text, rehearsing the oral part, looking up the meaning of slang expressions."

In the face of double standards, the women worked twice as hard. As a white woman leader said, "The only way that I know to overcome barriers is to do 150 percent, the very best job that I can." A Mexican American woman leader agreed:

> I have sometimes experienced the effects of being one of a very few Latinas in the legal profession. When I

*first started practicing, other attorneys thought I was
the court clerk and not the prosecutor. They attempted
to test my intelligence or my preparation, somehow
believing that since I was a minority woman, I might
not be as effective as my male Anglo counterparts. All
of this meant that I had to work harder and stay two
steps in front of them all.*

Women in the focus groups survived barriers of sexism and
racism in their own careers, but they were not able to remove
discriminatory practices from the workplace. A white woman
leader told us, "In spite of my achievements, I do not believe that
I have overcome these barriers because the next person coming
after me will have to deal with them." A Mexican American woman
leader agreed: "Some barriers could be overcome by persistence
and working harder; others could not be overcome." Approaching barriers with realism and hope, a white woman leader added:

*I have not overcome the barriers of prejudice, but I
continue to name them and bring them into the open.
I'd like to believe that most people are doing the best
they can in the world and that their homophobia or
racism or sexism will eventually give way to the vision and reality of a just world for all persons.*

What We Learned

Solo Status

Women in our focus groups were among the first women to lead
their human services organizations, an experience that psycholo-
gists call "solo status." As defined by Kathleen Hall Jamieson,
women are in solo status when they make up less than 15 percent to 25 percent of a management level. They are "at high risk
for stereotype appraisal" by clients, colleagues, and supervisors
from mainstream groups.[1] Monica Biernat and Diane
Kobrynowicz explain that in the dynamics of prejudice, women

in solo status are seen as "flowers blooming in winter," exceptional individuals whose achievements prove the stereotypical rule.[2] As a Puerto Rican woman leader remembered being told, "'You're not like other Puerto Ricans; you're an exception.'"

In the face of stereotypes, women in our focus groups tried to be good representatives of their social groups or communities, an ethical position that Stephanie Shaw calls "socially responsible individualism."[3] Various researchers have documented a sense of social responsibility among African American professional women, who are expected to "give back" to their community.[4] In a study of white women managers and black woman managers in corporations, Ella Bell and Stella Nkomo found that white women were more individualistic than black women managers, with little sense of responsibility to their communities or social groups.[5] In our focus groups, women from various racial and ethnic backgrounds expressed social identity and social responsibility. White women were less likely than women of color to identify with ethnic communities, but the white women leaders described responsibilities to other kinds of communities, such as "womankind"; lesbian, gay, bisexual, or transgender communities; or survivors of violence against women.[6] In the words of one white woman leader, "I am always carrying more than myself."

Glass Ceilings and Concrete Walls

Most research on women in management has been conducted in large corporations, where employment discrimination continues to block women's paths to senior management positions.[7] Stories from our focus groups reflect the reality of the glass ceiling and the concrete wall, discriminatory barriers that look much the same to women leaders in nonprofit organizations as to women managers in the corporate world.

One of the most comprehensive studies of employment discrimination in the United States was conducted by the Glass Ceiling Commission. Elizabeth Dole, who served as Secretary of Labor in the George H. W. Bush Administration, initiated an investigation into "artificial barriers to the advancement of women and minorities to management and decision-making positions in business."[8] The United States could not compete successfully in the global marketplace, Dole believed, without using the best skills and talents the U.S. workforce had to offer. Congress agreed. The Civil Rights Act of 1991 established the bipartisan Federal Glass Ceiling Commission, which studied the experiences of specific groups of workers: African American men, American Indian men, Asian Pacific American men, Latino men, and women. Its report, issued in 1995, came to an unequivocal conclusion:

> Equally qualified and similarly situated citizens are being denied equal access into senior level management on the basis of gender, race, or ethnicity. At the highest levels of corporations, the promise of reward for preparation and pursuit of excellence is not equally available to members of all groups. Furthermore it is against the best interests of business to exclude those Americans who constitute two-thirds of the total population, two-thirds of consumer markets, and more than half the workforce.[9]

The Federal Glass Ceiling Commission found that all women in corporate management experience barriers to advancement, but white women have made more progress than women from other racial and ethnic groups. Catalyst, a private research organization dedicated to the advancement of women in business, decided to find out why. Its 1999 report on *Women of Color in Corporate Management* complemented the work of the Federal Glass Ceiling Commission by analyzing the experiences of African American, Asian American, and Latina women.[10] As reported in these studies, women in corporate management, like women in our focus groups, face barriers of sexism and racism throughout their careers.

Senior managers in large corporations express commitment to diversity, but they understand diversity as recruiting like-minded people from different backgrounds. As one chief executive officer (CEO) explained, "What's important is comfort, chemistry in relationships . . . When we find minorities and women who think like we do, we snatch them up!"[11] Uncomfortable with difference, senior managers in corporations have "particularized prejudices," suspicions, and stereotypes about women and particular racial and ethnic groups.

In our focus groups, U.S.-born women and immigrant women described qualitatively different encounters with sexism and racism. In corporate settings, women from different racial and ethnic groups experience prejudice and discrimination in different ways. They describe their experiences in metaphors. Where white women see a glass ceiling, African American women find a steel vault or a concrete wall. Latinas work under an adobe ceiling, and Native Americans perceive a lower ceiling, thicker than glass. Asian Pacific Americans meet a bamboo ceiling or broken ladder, while a lavender ceiling restricts the career advancement of lesbian, bisexual, and transgender women.[12]

These metaphors depict cultural barriers. We cannot touch each other if separated by glass, but we cannot see each other from opposite sides of a concrete wall. To take the metaphors further, the most significant barriers to women in management are neither clear like glass nor opaque like adobe. They are stereotypes, trick mirrors that distort how we see each other. As described by a South Asian woman in our focus groups, "There is a difference between being seen as a curiosity and being seen as competent, being seen for who I am."

In relationships with colleagues, women in corporate management experience sexism and racism ranging from insensitive or ignorant remarks to incidents of sexual harassment. Like women in our focus groups, however, corporate women are less concerned by explicit expressions of prejudice than by implicit forms of bias. The Federal Glass Ceiling Commission found that senior managers in corporations make employment decisions on the basis of stereotypical views of women and of racial and ethnic groups. Double standards and biased rating and testing procedures are widely used.[13]

Women in our focus groups suspected that they were held to different, higher standards than men, and to judge by the corporate research, these suspicions were well founded. In one of our focus groups, for example, a Chinese American woman explained that she prepared extensively for oral presentations, because she was concerned that her accented English would make a bad impression. According to the Federal Glass Ceiling Commission, corporate managers use differential standards in judging communication skills. Employees who speak "Asian-accented English," in the commission's words, receive lower evaluations than employees with European accents or, for that matter, native English speakers, notwithstanding the quality of their English or the ability of listeners to understand what was said.[14] In response to vague evaluative criteria, women in corporations, like women in our focus groups, try to exceed expectations for any task.

Deep Structure

Business as usual often puts women at a disadvantage as a result of intentional or unintentional discriminatory practices. Researchers at the Center for Gender in Organizations locate discriminatory barriers in formal policies and procedures, in informal policies and procedures, and in the deep structure of organizations.[15] Formal policies may have discriminatory effects when qualifications for hiring or promotion, such as seniority or previous experience, are not necessary to succeed in the job. Informal policies and procedures may have discriminatory effects when they leave room for double standards in hiring, in compensating employees, and in evaluating work. In her research on employment discrimination, Barbara Reskin concluded that the greater the subjectivity in employment practices, the heavier the weight of prejudice and bias.[16]

Beyond formal and informal policies and procedures, discriminatory barriers are embedded in the "deep structure" of organizations. According to international researchers Aruna Rao and her colleagues, each organization has a deep structure, a "collection of values, history, culture, and practices that form the unquestioned, normal way of working."[17] Discriminatory barriers in the deep structure of organizations are the most difficult barriers to change. As described by a Puerto Rican woman leader in our focus groups, "Those barriers are hidden under the surface. Sometimes you're not aware of them; they are not in your face, but the opportunity somehow is not there for you."

We in the United States work together as we live together—in largely segregated worlds. The social patterns in organizations reflect the culture of the wider society, with its prejudices, expectations, and norms. According to sociologists Richard Zweigenhaft and William Domhoff, for example, the practice of holding meetings on the golf course has had significant discriminatory effects on women in corporate and political leadership.[18] When senior managers meet for a game of golf, they exclude those women managers and managers of color who do not play golf, who do not feel welcome in all-white country clubs, or who, in the case or women, have not been allowed to play at the same time as men. Similarly, when white men in senior management discuss work at social gatherings, they leave out other managers, often managers of color, who socialize with different groups of friends. Using their social networks to exchange professional news, to forge alliances, and to make plans, these managers protect their insider status, leaving women managers and managers of color in a position that Patricia Hill Collins calls the "outsider-within."[19]

Social patterns are replicated at home and at work, presenting different opportunities and obstacles for insider and outsider groups. In organizations as in households, women are more likely than men to perform "invisible work."[20] According to organizational researcher Joyce Fletcher, women managers are assigned responsibilities that are essential to organizations, such as facilitating teamwork, preparing for meetings, and representing the organization in the community. When they apply for promotions or raises, however, their work is not rewarded. As a white woman leader remembered, "The white straight guys were encouraged to do activities tied to promotion and tenure, while the rest of us did all the maintenance duties of the school."

Without insider information, women managers find it difficult to assess professional opportunities or to negotiate for compensation and resources comparable to those that men receive.[21] As a Puerto Rican woman leader claimed, "I have never been paid what I'm worth."

Women's difficulty in finding mentors exemplifies their status as "outsiders-within." According to Catalyst, "CEOs report having an influential mentor as the most significant factor in their own career advancement," but women in corporate management, particularly women managers of color, rarely find mentors to guide them.[22] Similarly, few women in our focus groups had mentors in their human services organizations. As a white woman leader recalled, "I've never had what I would call a mentor. I would call that a real missing piece."

Corporate researchers describe mentors as senior managers who contribute to the professional development of their mentees by sharing insiders' knowledge and skills. Mentors help mentees plan their careers by setting goals and identifying the skills and experiences that they need for advancement. They promote their mentees' accomplishments, sponsor them for visible assignments, and provide constructive criticism of their work.[23]

Senior managers in large corporations, most of whom are white men, usually mentor other white men or, less frequently, white women from socioeconomic backgrounds similar to their own. Both mentors and mentees generally prefer mentoring relationships with partners of the same sex, race, and ethnicity.[24] With relatively few women in senior management positions, the supply of women mentors, let alone women mentors from particular racial or ethnic groups of color, does not meet demand.

Researchers have found advantages in mentoring relationships between people of the same sex, race, and ethnicity. According to Michael Kelly and Kaitlin Post, mentoring relationships between women and men pose significant risks, both real and perceived. Colleagues may view male–female mentoring relationships with suspicion, imagining sexual overtones or favoritism. In mentoring relationships with men, women may feel vulnerable to sexual harassment or abuse of power.[25]

Race and ethnicity affect the quality of mentoring relationships, according to organizational research. In a Catalyst study of women managers of color, African American and Latina women felt that mentors of color, usually African American men, were more likely than white mentors to share their attitudes and values. Asian American women found mentors of color more likely than white mentors to have high expectations for their performance. In general, the women of color found mentors of color more caring and respectful of their goals.[26] Similarly, in a study of African American and white employees in a large utility company, David Thomas found that same-race mentoring relationships provided more psychosocial support than did cross-race relationships, although both types of relationships provided instrumental or practical career support.[27]

Breaking the Barriers

Giving credit where credit is due, researchers with the Federal Glass Ceiling Commission and Catalyst identified corporations that have improved recruitment and retention of women managers and managers of color. They cataloged "best practices," formal programs that guide women past barriers of discrimination.[28] More remedial than radical, many best practices help individuals compensate for discriminatory patterns without ending the discrimination.[29] Orientation programs and career planning services socialize women and managers of color to the organizational culture, teaching them the hidden rules. As part of orientation programs, formal mentors provide task-specific support to newcomers for a limited time.[30] Employee networks, such as women's networks or ethnic affinity networks, allow women and managers of color to find their own mentors and alliances within the organization. Women sometimes use employee networks as the means for social learning and more radical social action (see chapter 5).[31]

Some best practices, such as affirmative action and family-friendly policies, address formal policies and procedures, while other best practices, such as transparency in hiring, rewarding, and evaluating work, lessen the discriminatory effects of informal operations. Diversity training programs are popular best practices that are more successful in changing the behavior of individuals than in changing people's minds.[32] Like other best practices, they are slow to reach the deep structure of organizations.

Human services organizations, particularly large organizations or interagency coalitions, can adapt corporate best practices to human services environments. As leaders in human services, however, women in our focus groups were not satisfied with best practices that leave racism and sexism in place. They called for affirming diversity and promoting equity in their organizations and communities. They called for welcoming difference and learning from different points of view. They worked for social change at many levels: in themselves and other individuals, in organizations and communities, and in the relationships among them. As they overcame barriers to their own advancement, they never gave up hope of breaking the glass ceiling and the concrete wall.

৵৵৵

Summing Up Chapter 3: Themes from the Focus Groups

- African American, Mexican American, and Puerto Rican women leaders who were born in the United States became aware of racism in adolescence.
- African American parents tried to prepare the women for a racist world.
- South Asian women leaders experienced sexism as adolescents in India; they became aware of racial and ethnic stereotyping when they arrived in the United States.
- The women leaders could not always distinguish between racial and sexual discrimination as barriers to their advancement.
- Most were the first women or the first from their racial or ethnic groups to reach their professional positions.
- They were stereotyped or seen as exceptions to the rule.

- They tried to be good representatives of their social groups.
- They met differential standards by trying to do perfect work.
- They missed having mentors.
- They continue to fight against prejudice and discrimination in human services organizations.

ॐॐॐ

Action Steps

What Do You Think?

What barriers have you faced in your education and in your career? Which barriers are behind you? Which barriers will continue into the future? What strategies, resources, knowledge, and skills have you used in overcoming the obstacles in your path?

What Can You Do?

Wherever you are in your education or career, identify a woman who is following in your path, and reach out to her as a mentor. Alternatively, reach out as a peer mentor to a woman who is in an educational or professional position similar to yours. Offer to share information, friendship, ideas, advice, and introductions to colleagues in your field.

Where Can You Read More about Resisting Prejudice and Discrimination?

Catalyst. (1999b). *Women of color in corporate management: Opportunities and barriers*. NY: Author.

Daly, Alfreida (Ed.). (1998). *Workplace diversity: Issues and perspectives*. Washington, DC: NASW Press.

Woo, Deborah (2000). *Glass ceilings and Asian Americans: The new face of workplace barriers*. Walnut Creek, CA: AltaMira Press.

Chapter 4

∞

What Choices Did You Make?

"I am a value added."

<small>WOMEN LEADERS FOCUS GROUP</small>

A black leather jacket, a pair of exuberant earrings, a sari: On the way to leadership, the women in our focus groups had to decide what to wear. They formed their professional styles in the choices that they made throughout their careers. Sometimes they made choices that would change their lives, such as whether to marry, to have children, to move, or to respond to community needs. At other times, seemingly small choices of style—which clothing to wear, which language to speak, which issues to raise—took on larger meanings for the women, their communities, and their colleagues in human services organizations.

The Women's Stories

Moving between Worlds

Early in their lives, many women in our focus groups learned to move between different worlds. An African American woman leader remembered:

*It was in high school that I went into my black leather
jacket mode. You need to know that I was a wimp. I
had to walk through some bad neighborhoods, but I
knew how to walk like I knew what I was doing. I also
knew that when I got home, I needed to hide that little
leather jacket. It was this having to walk a different
walk in the neighborhood. It was being a tough black
kid when I wasn't. I quickly learned that I had to move
between these different worlds and still be acceptable
at some level in all of them, but just that notion of being able to move in and out of different cultures has
been something of a good.*

Women leaders used their skills in adapting to different cultures as they advanced in human services organizations. In organizations where all or nearly all the other managers were white
men, the women perceived themselves and were perceived as outsiders. Learning the language and customs of the organizational
culture, they balanced organizational expectations with their own
expectations, and they entered professional relationships while
maintaining community and family ties. Their challenge was to
lead with integrity, to hold on to essential values while moving
between worlds. As another African American woman leader
explained:

*Sure, I change behaviors and adapt to this setting or that
setting, but my core values are consistent. For example,
a core value is empathy. I monitor this in myself whether
I am dealing with my daughter, a colleague, a client, a
neighbor, or a person who is expressing a view that I
strongly disagree with.*

Women in our focus groups sought to be "included and counted,"
as a South Asian woman leader said, accepted and appreciated for
who they are. They expressed their identities as women and their
cultural heritage as a matter of professional style.

ॐ ॐ ॐ

Notes from Karen's Diary:
Style

As the first and only female academic dean in the history of the university, I struggled with how to look. How would my style enhance or diminish people's acceptance of me as a powerful person?

During my first year as dean, we convened a Futures Conference, inviting community leaders to help set priorities for social work education and practice. As I was deciding what to wear, I pulled out a pair of big, pretty earrings. My husband said definitively, "Those aren't professional!" I tried on little stud earrings and looked at myself in the mirror. "Well, these aren't me!"

I wore the big, fun earrings. Before the conference started, I had a laugh with somebody about this set of "high-level decisions." She then made our conversation part of her public introduction of me! At first, I felt very embarrassed. I feared that her introduction would diminish my credibility and power in the community, but in fact, it did just the opposite. It humanized me. Ever since then, people would look for my earrings and comment on them. Students and community people found it a nice way to approach me. They appreciated having a dean who was comfortable enough with herself to be fun and/or feminine, depending on what they saw. I was always careful, however. At a Board of Regents meeting or in certain areas where I thought the earrings would be distracting, I would choose differently.

As I became more comfortable with my own style, I found that I could use it to remind people of other differences that were more significant than the conversations we were having. I would sometimes use what I wore as a humorous reminder to my male colleague deans that, as much as I wanted to be one of the boys, I felt different and unique. My way of dressing symbolized differences in my values and perspectives, differences based on my being a woman and a social worker. My style allowed me to express who I am.

శ్రీశ్రీశ్రీ

The Best from Two Cultures

Women in our focus groups thought about how and when to fit into the mainstream. Their choices called attention to their diversity. A South Asian woman leader remembered:

> One of my earliest conscious resolutions soon after I came to this country was to integrate the best from the two cultures. I chose to dress in a manner that was comfortable and to continue wearing a sari. After all, my colleagues in academia were not tied to a dress code. This voluntary decision forced me to give endless explanations about saris. In my early starry-eyed years, I never suspected that in some cases, the questions had a very prejudicial bent. On one occasion, I fell on some ice on the ground. My colleague ran to the treasurer's office and warned him not to give me a workman's compensation claim if I asked for one, since I was wearing a sari and, in his view, that was what had caused me to fall.

An African American woman leader recalled:

> When I became dean, I can remember being with other women deans, white women. They would count the number of women deans, and I had to say, "I'm more

interested in the faces of color and, at this point, I have to say it doesn't matter to me whether those are male faces or female faces."

Lesbian women leaders balanced the risks and the rewards of revealing their sexual orientation, as a white woman leader explained:

Lesbians in leadership positions frequently don't talk about their personal lives or bring anyone with them to social events in order to protect their privacy. A norm evolves, and no one asks them about where they were on vacation or during holidays in order to respect their private lives. These were the kinds of models I had early in my career. I was "out" to all of my staff when I applied to be director, so they knew who they were getting. When I was offered the position, I used the opportunity to ask about domestic partnership benefits that were not available at the time. I have holiday parties at my home where my partner and our children are present, and I bring my family to all social events at work that include families. I think this has been a much healthier way to live my life.

Enriched

Women in various focus groups felt "enriched" by their cultural and bicultural experiences. For a South Asian woman leader,

Cultural difference provides a changed perspective and that changed perspective can be a great asset. It can be the cutting edge of a new idea or a new way of doing something.

To a Mexican American woman leader: "Each multicultural relationship helped make me a more open and accepting person." An African American woman leader agreed:

Now that I am grown, I can look back and see how enriching it has been to grow up and live in two worlds, one black and one white. As I matured and encountered other ethnic and cultural groups, I saw how many more worldviews there were. Even now, I meet others who believe that we are all on the same page with the same worldview. I hardly ever take for granted that my assumptions or worldviews reflect anyone else's. This gives me an ease with differences.

Another Mexican American woman leader explained:

Someone once said to me that racism and discrimination are the problems of the racist or discriminator, not the problems of the discriminated. I concur. Being of two cultures helped me when I practiced social work and enriched my career. I was able to be empathetic, to broker better, and to interpret verbal and nonverbal language.

Fluency in Spanish and English opened career opportunities for some women in our focus groups. A Puerto Rican woman leader remembered:

When I was six or seven, I was the family interpreter. I was the one who would deal with the bank tellers and the doctors, and this was my entrée into social work. Being bilingual/bicultural got me my first job as a case aide in a hospital. Later, when I was president of my professional association, I would always do a sound bite in Spanish, always make a bilingual statement about something. People would come up to me afterwards and say, "I am so proud of you." Usually, they were gray-haired little ladies who were just so touched. I always kept that in there, and it is part of who I am: enriched.

A Mexican American woman leader recalled:

I went to school at a time when students were being punished if they dared say anything in Spanish. I thought my Spanish language was going to hinder my education, but since my parents only spoke Spanish, I had no choice but to keep my Spanish-language ability strong. When I finally reached high school and realized that a second language would be needed to go on to college, I was ecstatic. I eventually majored in the language, and this has been a wonderful tool in all my different jobs, including serving on the city council. I led various trade missions for the city into Latin America.

Another Mexican American woman leader agreed:

I have used my Spanish-speaking abilities and my cultural awareness to open doors for my clients. My clients come from both the U.S. and Latin America. Trust is a big factor when clients are looking for an attorney and the ability to speak their language and know their customs has helped in achieving that trust.

So When's She Gonna Get Married?

Women in our focus groups were single, married, in domestic partnerships, widowed, divorced, parents, and nonparents. They had many kinds of families and family responsibilities. Some cared for children, and some cared for parents. Some lived near large extended families, and some had transnational families thousands of miles away. In nearly every family, however, the women's parents hoped that they would assume traditional family roles. A Puerto Rican woman leader remembered:

My mother knew I had a successful job, but still her friends would ask and she herself started to wonder, "So when is she gonna get married?" Now you've done all this and it's wonderful, but you've got to complete your

mission in life: Get married! And it was a long time be-
fore they stopped asking.

An African American woman leader added:

When I hit 40, my family stopped asking when I was
getting married. They started saying, "She's too smart to
get married," to make it okay.

Another Puerto Rican woman leader reflected:

I still feel the struggle to deal with my mother and other
folks who identify success with those traditional kinds
of things. My husband and I made a conscious choice
not to have children. People think, "Oh, poor you," or
"Something's wrong with you." We were the first gen-
eration who could make that conscious choice. It wasn't
an easy choice, but it was a choice for our careers and
for what we wanted to do with our lives.

The African American woman leader replied:

I don't know how I feel about not having children. I
think that women who have never borne children are
looked at in a very different way. We get segregated at
the table at family gatherings. There's this thing that
women who have children share and talk about, and those
who don't have children are left out.

The women leaders who were parents balanced family and professional responsibilities in various ways. Some took time out from
careers and cared for children at home. Some began college or returned to graduate school while their children were young. Others
combined full-time employment with homemaking and child care.
A Chinese American woman leader recalled:

I chose to stay at home to raise my children for 10 years. Of course, when it came time to look for a professional position, the gap in my résumé was a liability! Voluntary community service and travel did not count with employers, who had hundreds of applicants to choose from.

A white women leader remembered her struggles as a single parent:

My husband died when my children were small. I had to earn a living, so I went back to work, and I also went on for my doctorate. My parents were very helpful, but it was difficult. While I was writing my dissertation, my son called it "the thing" because there were lots of things we weren't able to do. We weren't able to go here on Saturday and there in the summer because of "the thing." So it's difficult, and I empathize with people who are struggling in the same way.

An African American woman leader found help with domestic responsibilities:

When I had my first child, I was in an important position in my career. A friend advised me, "You are not perfect, and you can't do everything alone. Give your attention to what you feel is most important, and get help when you need it." Over the years, my husband increased his role in the care of the boys, and we hired someone to help with the house. I organized my professional schedule so that I could handle the kids' activities.

While some women balanced professional and domestic work with help from family or paid employees, South Asian women leaders did it all on their own. "It's a very big burden that South Asian women carry," they explained:

There are cultural expectations on South Asian women. The way you are brought up, even though achievement and education and a career are emphasized and encouraged, there is always that other message that you have to be a good mother and a good wife and a good home-maker. Basically, you have to become a superwoman. You struggle with it, but each of us contributes to that community pressure by trying to do it all and not freeing ourselves from community expectations.

Another South Asian woman leader remembered:

At one time, I was taking care of a sick mother and two kids under the age of six, taking all three of them out in the morning and then bringing them back in the evening and having a traveling husband. Sometimes I was extremely overwhelmed with the work. If I look back, what I would have done differently was teach our generation of husbands to do more work at home. It's difficult after 15, 20 years of marriage to tell them, "Start doing new chores!"

Women in our focus groups remembered family responsibilities as both stressful and supportive. Experiences in families enhanced professional skills. A white woman leader reflected:

Certainly, having daughters deepened my commitment and passion to end violence against women. My scholarship may have lost out in terms of quantity and my teaching may not have had as many typed pages of notes, but once I felt comfortable with my multiple roles, quality was enhanced as quantity diminished.

Another white woman leader agreed:

The life experience provided by all these roles and commitments contributed to my growth and my professional capacities. I had plenty of practice in learning to prioritize time, honor values, balance commitments, set limits, pay attention to myself and others, empathize, encourage, take care of myself and not get lost, and study human development—both child and adult development, including my own! I also had plenty of opportunity to fail at those things and to learn to do them better.

Where You Are in Life

As they balanced their responsibilities in their families and communities, the women leaders chose whether to relocate for the sake of their careers. Some women decided to move to new jobs, while others passed up career opportunities rather than uproot their families or live apart from them. In deciding whether to move, they weighed the relative degrees of prejudice, particularly racism or homophobia, that they might find in another part of the United States. An African American woman leader explained:

There are certain limitations to what you can do because of where you are in life. It may be that if you have young children, you cannot move. It may be that your husband or partner cannot move, and therefore you are limited in your choices. Even health can be a barrier to doing certain things. In addition, minority women have barriers. There are places you don't go. And yet there may be wonderful opportunities there for career advancement. My family couldn't understand why in the world I, a black woman, would go to Alabama. "The reason you were born in Boston is because we left the South!"

A lesbian woman leader was limited to states that would give legal recognition to her family:

In the state where I live and work now, my university provides domestic partnership benefits to gay and lesbian families, and my family is legally recognized. That would not be possible in all states. In some states, I would not be allowed to adopt the children I have been raising for the past 10 years. I would live in fear that my children could be taken away from me. I would not be allowed to live openly with my partner and keep my job. I would not be able to speak out about increasing health care benefits and other benefits for my family. I have received many requests to apply for positions at other institutions, but in this respect, I am limited in my advancement.

The Pull of Community

Beyond their families and their careers, women in our focus groups felt "the pull of the community." An African American woman leader remembered:

As a brand-new faculty member, freshly graduated from a doctoral program and relocated to Houston, I felt the pull of the community. The choice was mine: to respond or not to respond. I chose to respond. I could not devote myself solely to writing and research, although I was constantly advised to do just that in order to qualify for tenure. Instead, I had to establish community contact, to make a meaningful contribution, to be involved. I could not forget where I came from and just do my own egocentric thing.

A Mexican American woman leader wished for a role model to help her balance professional responsibilities with community service:

One of my deepest regrets is that I have yearned for role models that are Hispanic or Latina professionals and have been unable to find them. I struggled when Hispanic friends told me that I needed to be in the barrio working with the community, thus leaving me with a feeling that I had abandoned my people.

However, an African American woman leader was not always ready for her role model's call:

> I spent some time with a woman who has become a mentor in recent years. She decided that she needed to take me under her wing. She is this wonderful lady who is saying to me, "Your work is never done." When she calls, I think, "Oh, no, here's Mrs. B., and what does she want me to do now?" I had dinner with her a few Sundays ago. She's just shy of 80, and she's almost shaking with this: "There's so much to do! Look how bad it is! Isn't anybody paying any attention?" And I feel so guilty. I love being with her, but I don't have the energy. She sees me as someone who's positioned to do these things that she has not been able to finish, and now I must do it. I mean, always a new assignment. And I want to say, "Please just pass the chicken, and let me go home!"

A Value Added

In the end, women in our focus groups were satisfied with their choices. In the words of a Mexican American woman leader, "I always did and gave the very best with no regrets." As mentors to future leaders, they advised women to be true to themselves. An African American woman leader reflected:

> It takes some doing to help minority women feel that they bring something of value to the table. I often say to my students, "When you apply for a position, you may feel so grateful that someone is interested enough in you to give you a job, particularly in a white institution. But you must turn to them and say, 'I am a value added. I bring something to the table beyond just a newly minted PhD,' and begin to negotiate out of success."

A white lesbian woman leader gave this advice:

To lesbian women who are prospective leaders: Know that you will have unique, additional demands on your time and energy because you don't fit the mold of heterosexuality or the mold of "the guys" in leadership. Know that you will be faced with thousands of small, yet painful, reminders of your "difference." Consistently educate colleagues and they will work to educate others. Develop a circle of supportive friends to whom you can speak candidly; don't rely solely on your partner for support. Recognize that no one can tell you how you should be in the leadership world. Listen to the stories of other women as guides; use what is helpful and discard the rest. Forgive yourself for the times you have compromised yourself too much; there will be many opportunities to do it differently.

Another white woman leader advised:

I encourage each woman to be more of herself and not to try to be exactly like she perceives men to be in leadership roles, to take the best of more masculine role modeling and to discard the worst. I encourage each woman to ignore and transcend the "way things have always been done." What's so good about how they've always been done? Why not do them some other way, some way that looks reasonable to her, whether or not it's the way a man would insist things must be done? If you're going to subject yourself to the stresses of being a woman leader, you might as well make it count. Do something different!

What We Learned

Work–Family Balance

Can women have it all, both families and careers? Can women succeed as mothers and managers at the same time? "Work–family balance" remains a hot topic in organizational research. As recently as 2002, a book by economist Sylvia Ann Hewlett, which warned women not to delay motherhood for the sake of careers, made the cover of *Time*, *The New York Times*, and television network news.[1]

Much research on work–family balance is based on the experiences of white, middle-class families.[2] As women struggle to provide child care, eldercare, and housework while pursuing professional goals, they perceive family and career as competing for their time. From this perspective, the more time and attention women give to their families, the less they have for their careers.

When researchers define "family" as parents and children living in the same household, or when they imply that "having a family" means "having children," they see work–family balance from a narrow point of view. When researchers expand their studies to include the experiences of women from various racial and ethnic groups, they discover complementary as well as competitive dynamics in the relationship between family and work. Sumru Erkut, a researcher with Wellesley College Center for Research on Women, surveyed 60 multicultural women leaders in various fields.[3] Women leaders in her study believed that family responsibilities contributed to their professional advancement, because they learned leadership skills in their roles as mothers and older sisters.

Patricia Hill Collins, in her research on African American families, suggested that motherhood may prepare black women for professional leadership roles.[4] Anthropologists Catherine Medina and Gaye Luna found that Latina professional women emulate their own mothers' leadership skills. As Medina and Luna explained, "The mothers and mother-images for Latina women have traditionally been dynamic and determined women who have prevailed over their own societal obstacles."[5] Internationally, motherhood has inspired women to organize movements for social change. "Activist mothers" led community development programs in low-income urban neighborhoods, founded Mothers Against Drunk Driving (MADD) in the United States, staged antinuclear demonstrations in Mexico, and held protest marches in Argentina in memory of "the disappeared."[6]

Like "activist mothers," women in our focus groups did not draw clear boundaries between family and community. Maintaining close relationships with their extended families, including transnational families, they struggled to meet their many responsibilities at home, in their communities, and in the workplace. As a South Asian woman leader remembered, "Sometimes I was extremely overwhelmed with the work." Even when family and work competed for their attention, however, the women leaders perceived family relationships as complementing their professional lives.

When they were children, the women learned cultural wisdom from their families, including knowledge, skills, and values that they later applied in their careers (see chapter 2). When they reached adulthood, they gained leadership experience in their family and community roles. Some women in our focus groups learned leadership skills as mothers, but regardless of whether they had children, the women leaders assumed responsibilities as role models for families and communities. An African American woman leader discovered that "we are role models for persons we don't even know."

In addition to learning leadership skills in their families and communities, some women in our focus groups gained experience in effecting social change. Mexican American, Puerto Rican, and South Asian women leaders remembered mediating between the cultural traditions of older generations and the values of younger generations. Through their own professional choices, they introduced changes in their families' expectations of women.[7] Their experiences as change agents in families and communities may have prepared the women leaders to work for change in human services organizations, where they mediated between the traditions of mainstream human services professions and the values and needs of multiethnic client communities.[8]

Bicultural Paths

Some women in our focus groups entered the United States as immigrants, some grew up in ethnic U.S. communities, and some identified as part of the white, majority culture. Although they came from different backgrounds, all the women followed bicultural or multicultural paths to leadership in human services. As the first women in their professional roles, they were strangers in strange and sometimes hostile organizational cultures. Moving between worlds of their families, their communities, and their organizations, they made conscious choices about how much to conform to the expectations of mainstream managers, who were predominantly white men. When and how would they live by organizational expectations? When and how would they express different values and points of view?

As described by the Federal Glass Ceiling Commission, the women leaders faced "particularized" prejudices against their racial, ethnic, and social groups, and historical experience may have influenced their responses to discrimination.[9] According to researchers Margaret Gibson and John Ogbu, for example, "voluntary minorities," such as first-generation immigrant and migrant groups, view biculturality with greater optimism and hope than "involuntary minorities," who remember generations of oppression.[10]

Women leaders from ethnic groups of color had many cultural boundaries to cross.[11] Jeanette Jennings, Ruth R. Martin, and Phyllis Ivory Vroom described their own experiences as African American administrators in schools of social work.[12] They served as "boundary spanners," reaching across the boundaries of the wider society, the African American community, and the community of black women. From the cultural margins of their organizations and communities, they experienced social isolation, challenges to their credibility, and assaults on their ethics and values.[13]

Women in our focus groups remembered similar challenges as they moved between cultures. In the words of a South Asian woman leader, "Sometimes you don't know where you belong." Whatever their race or ethnicity, however, the women leaders understood their bicultural or multicultural experiences as assets to their careers. Bicultural awareness gave them an "ease with differences," perceptions of "new ways" of doing things, and opportunities "to open doors for clients." They valued their skills in relating to various communities and, as boundary spanners, in building bridges among them.

According to ethnic identity theory, cultural values have a protective function for ethnic communities that face prejudice in the greater society.[14] Women in our focus groups may have been similarly protected from bicultural stress by their sense of social purpose. Having entered human services to "make a positive difference," they integrated personal, cultural, and professional values and goals, such as the value of appreciating diversity and the goal of ending prejudice and discrimination. A Mexican American woman leader found, "I have been able to integrate personal, cultural, and professional values and goals by not losing sight of where I came from." A Puerto Rican woman leader agreed:

> I entered the profession of social work through a series of relationships, mentoring relationships, organizations that I belonged to, and my work was never different or isolated from my community activity. I carried into my place of work my sense of belonging in a community. I have been so privileged. I have always worked at something that, had I not been paid, I would have done anyway.

The women leaders traveled between their "communities of identity" at home and their professional communities at work without losing themselves along the way.[15] Using a process called "selective assimilation," they chose cultural styles that met their needs in particular places and times.[16] An African American women leader, for example, remembered going into her "black leather jacket mode" to fit into her neighborhood on the way to school. Another African American woman leader explained, "Sure, I change behaviors and adapt to this setting or that setting, but my core values are consistent."

Early in their careers, the women leaders chose conformist styles that helped them adapt to their professions and organizations. As they advanced into leadership positions, they sometimes chose nonconformist professional styles as a means for resisting prejudice and discrimination. They wore "cultural markers," such as ethnic jewelry; used gestures and expressions from their heritage languages; and explicitly protested against discrimination.[17] As a white woman leader ruefully observed, "My vocal expressions of concern for social justice for women, people of color, and lesbian and gay people haven't always helped my career."

These acts of resistance were also acts of empowerment for the women leaders. Social work researchers Lorraine Gutiérrez and Edith Lewis identified three dimensions to empowerment: building confidence, raising consciousness, and building connections.[18] Through nonconformist choices of style, women in our focus groups expressed confidence and pride in their cultural identities, called attention to diversity, and reached out to others from their social groups. A Puerto Rican woman leader empowered herself and other Latino/Latina social workers when she spoke in Spanish to her professional association: "I would always do a sound bite in Spanish . . . it's a part of who I am: enriched."

Prevailing Wisdom

While women in our focus groups empowered themselves through nonconformist professional styles, management consultants advised women to conform to the corporate world. In the late 1960s and the 1970s, women began entering male-dominated professions in unprecedented numbers. In business as in child care, experts were ready to give women advice. Self-help books for women in corporate management instructed women to "dress for success," to act assertively—but not too assertively—and to play by rules developed by and for the predominant groups of white men in power.[19]

The conformist approach to professional advancement remains popular today. In *Play Like a Man, Win Like a Woman*, Gail Evans offers a chapter on "six things men can do at work that women can't: cry, have sex, fidget, yell, have bad manners, or be ugly."[20] In "Bully Broads," a professional development seminar for women managers, Jean A. Hollands trains executive women to give up aggressive behavior for more traditional feminine ways.[21] To social work educators Lynne Healy, Catherine Havens, and Barbara Pine, self-help literature remains "an insidious obstacle to women's progress" that presents women's ways of communicating and relating to others as wrong.[22]

Like popular literature, much scholarly literature on women in management has looked to the behavior of women, rather than the behavior of organizations, as a barrier to women's advancement.

Some writers assume, for example, that a "feminine style of communicating" limits women's effectiveness in negotiating with men.[23] In a major study of negotiations, researchers Deborah Kolb and Judith Williams found that women were disadvantaged not by their communication styles but by their lack of access to informal networks and conversations among people in power. By the time women get to the negotiating table, the decisions have already been made.[24]

Organizational researcher Robin Ely agrees that scholarly research on gender in organizations is more likely to focus on the psychology of women than on the social, economic, or political practices of organizations. After reviewing 57 empirical research articles in major academic journals, Ely concluded that researchers "did not address the unequal distribution of power between men and women, nor the ways in which organizations, through their unexamined policies, procedures, and norms, uphold that unequal distribution."[25]

Much literature on women in management, like literature on work–family balance, has generalized from the experiences of white, middle-class women. In her survey of empirical research, Ely found that researchers understand gender in organizations as a white woman's issue. They rarely consider the implications of race, ethnicity, socioeconomic status, or sexual orientation on women's careers.[26] As South African researcher Nozipho January-Bardill explains, "Many still resist the notion that while women may all be sitting on the same boat, black and working-class women may be sitting on different decks."[27]

While literature on women managers has focused on the behavior of individual women, a parallel stream of literature on managing diversity has targeted organizational behavior for change. Until recently, much research on women managers considered sexism from the perspectives of white women, while research on managing diversity viewed racism from the perspectives of men. In what Ruby Marks and her colleagues called the "hierarchy of oppressions," researchers have found it difficult to confront issues of race, sex, and class at the same time.[28] Ultimately, what women leaders need is research that explores how the choices of individual women affect organizational practices and how organizational practices affect different groups in different ways.

Women in our focus groups considered how their choices would affect their families, their communities, and their organizations. They viewed their career paths from a "life course perspective," in the words of gerontologists Eleanor Palo Stoller and Rose Campbell Gibson.[29] Race, ethnicity, sex, sexual orientation, national origin, religion, disability, and age were all parts of the women leaders' stories. In addition, they identified opportunities and obstacles in the historical times when they grew up, in the places where they lived, and in the relationships that they cultivated throughout their careers.

Learning to lead from their families, communities, and professions, they remembered where they came from while trusting in the possibilities for social change. As a Mexican American woman leader reflected:

> *Family, faith, and friends have kept me rooted, and the world of academe has given me wings. I could not be where I am today without having both a sense of roots and a sense of freedom to explore new avenues, new technology, and new ways of doing things.*

ᔥᔥᔥ

Summing Up Chapter 4:
Themes from the Focus Groups

- Women in our focus groups held on to "core values" while adapting to different environments.
- They expressed their social identities, such as their cultural heritage or their identities as women, through their professional styles.
- They spoke out against prejudice and discrimination.
- Cultural and bicultural awareness were professional assets that helped them communicate, accept differences, and perceive new ways of doing things.
- Fluency in Spanish opened career opportunities.
- The women leaders had many kinds of families and family responsibilities.

- They responded to the pull of the community.
- Racism and homophobia limited their geographic mobility.
- Family and community responsibilities were both stressful and supportive for the women leaders.
- They learned skills in leadership and in effecting social change from their family roles.
- They advised younger women to be true to themselves.

ৡৡৡ

Action Steps

What Do You Think?

What leadership skills have you learned from your family? Consider leadership skills that you have observed in women in your family and leadership experience that you have gained in your own family roles. Which of these skills are effective in leading human services? How is leading a family similar to and different from leading a human services organization?

What Can You Do?

Identify your personal and professional goals for the next five years and the barriers and opportunities that you may face. Make a tentative five-year plan for overcoming barriers and realizing opportunities in reaching your personal and professional goals.[30]

Where Can You Read More about Professional Women's Choices?

The Latina Feminist Group. (2001). *Telling to live: Latina Feminist Testimonios*. Durham, NC: Duke University Press.

Reid-Merritt, Patricia (1996). *Sister power: How phenomenal black women are rising to the top*. New York: John Wiley & Sons.

Wu, Diana Ting Liu Wu (1997). *Asian Pacific Americans in the workplace*. Walnut Creek, CA: AltaMira Press.

Chapter 5

֍

Where Did You Find Support?

"I can't imagine how women make it without strong women friends."

WOMEN LEADERS FOCUS GROUP

It took courage to be the first women or the first from their racial or ethnic groups to lead their organizations, but if the women leaders were on their own, they rarely felt alone. As a Mexican American woman leader explained, "I draw on tremendous support from my loved ones, friends, colleagues, and my spirituality, so I actively seek this support and draw from my other masters in life." Another Mexican American woman leader agreed:

I would advise all to be aware that we are not alone in this work. There are others, and it is important to network in a formal or informal manner. We all need support, whether it is from loved ones or professional colleagues.

For an African American woman leader:

77

My challenge has not been loneliness, but rather too much connection, too many people to try and keep up with, too much to do. I have had to learn to cut back and cut down so that I could have a more balanced life and spend more time with the people I love. This is still my challenge.

Women in our focus groups valued their relationships. Their capacities for entering into and sustaining relationships allowed them to advance professionally, to lead effectively, and to hold on to their values and goals.

The Women's Stories

Relationships

Women in our focus groups did not distinguish between personal and professional relationships as resources for their careers. They found emotional support from colleagues, and they learned professional skills from family and friends. A Mexican American woman leader said:

Relationships are highly important to me, and this is quite related to my culture as a Mexican American. I have been taught that relationships are the most important thing in life. My continued success in social work has a lot to do with relationships I have had along the way. My first and foremost support person has been my mother. She had a beautiful way of instilling this sense of belief in me and in anything that I undertook in life. I have met others in my professional and personal life that have been able to instill these same feelings as well. My support persons or networks have not been formal groups, but rather small clusters of good and intimate colleagues that I can turn to in times of need.

An African American woman leader also enjoyed many sources of support:

> *Since I began college, I have been a part of networks, groups, and mentoring relationships. All have helped me to succeed and also advised and listened when I may have been on the wrong path. These relationships included supervisors at work, professors, sorority sisters, the Association of Black Social Workers, church members, neighbors, best friends from high school, and I could go on and on. The most important aspect of these relationships has been to provide me feedback and support on call. There has never been a time I've ever had to want for a kind ear or a helping hand.*

The women leaders remembered childhood relationships in their families and communities as the sources of professional knowledge, skills, and values (see chapter 2). "From the very first moment of my life, my relationship to my mother, father, sisters, and brothers laid the foundation of who I was to become," said an African American woman leader. Most women in our focus groups had been inspired by their mothers. Another Mexican American woman leader reflected, "As my mother provided the inspiration, my friends have provided the linkages and networks so necessary to a professional."

Many women leaders entered human services through community organizations when they were adolescents or young adults. "The community is where you emerged from," explained an African American woman leader. As they moved to new communities and new countries, married and entered domestic partnerships, explored new interests, and advanced in their careers, the women leaders kept in touch with childhood friends. Another African American woman leader remembered:

> *I am fortunate to have a large extended family and several friends whom I have known for decades, over 20, 30, even 40 years. When I felt like the only, I would*

*call up my friends around the country who were also
"onlies" in their professions. When I wanted a support network of people whose interests paralleled mine,
I joined the Organizational Development Network and
eventually founded an organization that specialized in
organizational development for nonprofits.*

A Chinese American woman leader recalled:

*I have an international network of women friends who
date from my teen years in Hong Kong. Several of them
were my classmates from seventh grade through college. Several were friends from my church youth group.
We are in Canada, Hong Kong, Australia, and the U.S.
and use faxes, e-mail, and phone calls to communicate.
When I began teaching social work in the U.S., I also
worked extremely hard to develop a network with my
professional colleagues, first locally, then nationally.*

For a Mexican American woman leader:

*Relationships include my circle of girlfriends who come
together to encourage and pray for all our lives. Friends
from high school, college, and law school get together
at least once or twice a year. I have professional relationships that assist in identifying opportunities for
me to speak or network. And my best one is my relationship to my husband, who has come through as a
true partner.*

Strong Women Friends

Some women leaders described supportive relationships with
male colleagues, and some married women leaders felt supported
by their husbands or partners, but nearly all the women leaders
relied on "strong relationships with women" for support. As a
white woman leader remembered:

I could not have survived the battered women's shelter movement, masters or doctoral programs, or my career in higher education without strong, healthy relationships with women who cared about me and cared about the issues for which I had such passion. Through networks, I have felt able to call upon people with feelings of trust when I have had serious concerns. Relationships have helped! They have challenged me to do more and to do it better. They have sustained me and nurtured me. They have shown me gentleness when others were showing arrogance or domination.

Another white woman leader found:

Relationships have kept me going in my career. If it were not for the strong feminist network I have outside the university, I might have begun to believe the patriarchal constructs were correct! My partner has been a major support over the past 19 years we have been together. Now I receive much support as well from younger women I have mentored and from young, feminist men who are former students.

An African American woman leader added:

I can't imagine how women make it without strong women friends. I have longtime friends from 30 years back all around the country with whom I keep up via e-mail and visits. In addition to my friends, I belong to a dialogue group of men and women. We meet together about nine times a year. All of us are in the same field of practice, organizational behavior and change, so we address personal issues from that vantage point. I also turn to various professionals. I have people available to help me help others as well as myself.

As the first women from their racial or ethnic groups in an organization, the women leaders formed multicultural coalitions. A Puerto Rican woman leader recalled:

> *My teachers were mostly Jewish social workers, and they've been a very integral part of my life. Also, I would join the African American group when there was no other association to join. When I was in graduate school, there was only the Black Student Association, so I joined it. I made the translation from the African American experience to the Latino experience. Today, there is a lot written about all different cultural groups, but when I was starting out, I had to be the expert. I had to teach myself my culture and a lot of other cultures, too.*

A Missing Piece

In these rich systems of support, a few women leaders found mentors, more experienced, senior professionals who guided them as they advanced in their careers. A white woman leader recalled:

> *I was very blessed with two wonderful mentors. The first one was my first supervisor. I worked for a child advocacy agency, and this woman was so talented. Most of what I learned about social work I learned from her. Then there was a colleague who worked with me in that agency at a senior level. She left the agency to go into teaching, and she began to engage me in social work education of students in the field. I'm eternally grateful for both of them, and as an agenda, it is my own desire to pay back and mentor others in their professional careers.*

A Mexican American woman leader also felt grateful to her mentor:

An important relationship was with a bilingual, bicul-
tural female attorney. She was from Venezuela and
had immigrated to the U.S. with her husband and three
children, and she had to start law school all over again.
She said if she could do it, I, too, could go to law
school with two kids in tow. I had my last child in
my last year of law school, three months before the
bar exam.

Most women in our focus groups did not have mentors, however. Mentors did not reach out to the women leaders, and in
some cases, the women did not reach out to mentors. Prejudice
and stereotyping may have prevented senior managers from noticing the potential of women to advance into leadership positions (see chapter 3). "Comfort with the familiar" or discomfort
with the unfamiliar may have prevented men from mentoring
women with racial, ethnic, or social backgrounds different
from their own. As a white woman leader observed, "Mentoring
in my school varied, depending upon race, gender, and sexual
orientation."

At the same time, experiences with sexism, racism, and employment discrimination prevented some women from seeking
mentors. As objects of stereotyping, they had fought for credibility. They had learned not to ask for help. An African American woman leader explained:

Being a product of affirmative action, there's a part of
me that always says, "Am I perceived as someone who
has any talent, or am I perceived mainly as someone
who benefited from affirmative action?" I have had
to learn to seek out assistance. People have assumed a
level of competency and accomplishment. They haven't
said, "Gee, you seem to be floundering over there; let
me help." I put the energy into not appearing to be
floundering. I have had to develop a level of comfort
in saying, "You know, I really would like to talk to

you about how you managed these different things,"
and feeling that would be okay without people say-
ing, "Uh huh, she really is an affirmative action
appointment."

What women leaders missed in mentors—guidance, information, encouragement, and sponsorship—they found in each other
through formal and informal networks and professional groups.
They became "peer mentors" to other women in their situations.
As an African American woman put it, "When I felt like the only,
I would call up my friends around the country who were also
'onlies' in their professions." A white woman leader explained:

> *Before beginning graduate school, I came out as les-*
> *bian. Networking in that community has definitely*
> *been useful in my career because many of my referrals*
> *come from that community. I made a number of very*
> *good friends during graduate school and we have be-*
> *come a professional network, providing mutual con-*
> *sultation for each other in group settings. I've never*
> *had what I would call a mentor. I would call that a*
> *real missing piece. On the other hand, I have had the*
> *support of many women friends and colleagues who*
> *are my peers, and that has been extremely valuable.*

Networks and Groups

The women leaders established bonds with other women in formal and informal networks and professional groups, and through
the years, they advanced together into more senior leadership
positions. They continued to rely on one another for mutual aid,
including practical information, advice, and emotional support.
As the first women in their positions, they felt a responsibility to
other women and to women from their racial and ethnic groups.
As participants in their networks, they felt part of something
greater than themselves. An African American woman leader
reflected:

I have often been the "only one," but time has brought about many changes. The Association of Black Social Workers and other such groups were a strong source of support. There have been many women historically in this field. They paved the way and made it easier to negotiate the profession for people like me. When I became senior vice president at the United Way, there were at least 10, 15 women like myself across the country that I could call on. When I became president of the Urban League, I was joined at the same time by at least 10 other women. Today, 50 percent of the 114 Urban League presidents from across the country are women.

A white woman leader recalled:

The national relationships that I have formed with women have been very, very important to me. They helped me think about important issues and various views on the issues, and, of course, they've opened further doors always. If things are difficult at times in my own work, in a way it balances because I have my national colleagues. It doesn't matter too much if we don't see each other very frequently because we continue to see each other over many years and have important discussions.

The Next Generation

Women in our focus groups appreciated the meaning of their work to other women, and they assumed responsibilities as role models to younger women in their families, communities, and professions. As an African American woman leader said, "We help other women advance by the role models we are." Another African American woman leader reflected:

I find it very rewarding and humbling when a young person will say, "It never occurred to me that you were

*a black woman!" And the meaning that it has to her!
I never think of myself like that. I just work real hard;
I'm doing all right if I don't get fired by the end of the
week. And then another young African American person comes and just because you're there, it makes a
whole difference in their lives.*

A Mexican American woman leader discovered:

*Without my even noticing, other women have been
following along, setting their own goals. We impact
whether we realize it or not. Others do see our accomplishments. Most women just need a little affir-
mation or confirmation that what they are doing
matters or that they are on the right path. We do have
a responsibility to reach out.*

Another African American woman leader found:

*Sometimes I receive comments from young women and
even men who have known my work. Because of what
they knew about me, they were encouraged to make
career and professional decisions that they might not
have considered otherwise. We are role models for
persons we don't even know.*

As they advanced into leadership positions, women in our
focus groups reached out as mentors to younger women. A white
woman leader explained:

*I try to help younger women by being available, shar-
ing information with them, telling about my experiences, connecting them to resources, and encouraging
them to expand their world by trying something they
haven't already tried. And most importantly, I advise
them to be sure to stay connected with other professionals that they admire and respect.*

A Mexican American woman leader advised:

> We are all incredible human beings with many talents, gifts, experience, knowledge, and wisdom. My advice is to share these attributes with others. One must be more proactive in reaching out to help those who are unfamiliar: Send them information. Help those who need recommendations: Write letters on their behalf. Help those who are struggling with career choices: Tell them how you resolved your own decisions. Help those who need the benefit of the doubt: Encourage them to take risks and let them know you'll be there for them should they need help. And above all pray for your relationships: Pray for their growth in wisdom, pray for their success, and pray that they be protected.

What We Learned

Nothing Living Lives Alone

Women in our focus groups gave and received support through an array of relationships. They treasured their friendships, maintaining early ties to families and communities, while also reaching out to new communities and professional groups. As their social systems expanded, so did their capacities and skills as leaders. With many people believing in them, they could hold on to their optimism, self-confidence, and willingness to take risks. With relationships in many communities, they could observe the world from various points of view. Their commitment to social change arose from relationships that, in turn, provided the political backing to accomplish their goals.

The women leaders shared what organizational theorist Margaret Wheatley called a systems perspective, the understanding that "nothing living lives alone."[1] Human beings, like other life forms, survive in "a web of relationships," as Wheatley explained, growing and changing in relation to all other living things in a system. In the professional world, as in the natural world, every relationship matters, and no relationship can be confined to a predictable purpose, place, or time.

With their systems perspective, the women leaders did not rank relationships in order of importance or categorize people into separate parts of their lives. In giving support to others, they were not hoping for a *quid pro quo*, a favor to themselves. Rather, they hoped to benefit a greater whole. As a Mexican American woman leader said, "I have often been given favors by others. I repay this by granting the favor back to the next person that needs it."

To sustain their many relationships, the women learned to balance commitments, manage time, and set realistic expectations for their relationships and for themselves. Another Mexican American woman leader advised:

> *We all need balance. Talented people stay busy and overwhelmed, and they often talk about what they will do when they have free time. However, the free time doesn't come unless we carefully and thoughtfully plan for it.*

The women leaders' approach to relationships was based on their experiences in families and communities, their cultural values, and their solo status in human services organizations. In the words of one woman leader, "Relationships are highly important to me, and this is quite related to my culture as a Mexican American." Their relational capacities and skills may also be attributed to their psychological development as women or their socialization into traditional gender roles.

Women's Development

During the second wave of feminism in the 1970s and 1980s, researchers discovered developmental patterns in women that had not been documented in earlier research on men. In studying psychological development, Nancy Chodorow found that girls develop a basis for empathy in their relationships with their mothers. As they form their sexual identities in early childhood, girls do not need to separate themselves from their primary caregivers in the same way as boys.[2] Jean Baker Miller reasoned further that girls and women develop their relational skills as a means of surviving oppression.[3] In studying women's moral development, Carol Gilligan noted that girls and women are often more concerned with sustaining relationships than with upholding abstract principles of justice.[4] Educational researchers Mary Belenky, Blythe Clinchy, Nancy Goldberger, and Jill Tarule wrote that some women use empathy when confronted with new ideas. In a phase of educational development called "connected learning," they imagine what it would be like to agree with the new idea rather than arguing against it.[5] Philosopher Nel Noddings articulated a "feminine approach to ethics" based on women's experiences in caring for many types of relationships as they fill multiple roles.[6]

Researchers today are using developmental theory to learn about the relational skills of women leaders. At the Stone Center at Wellesley College, Judith Jordan and her colleagues have proposed a relational–cultural model as a way to understand how women give and receive support.[7] Jean Baker Miller and Irene Stiver identified relationships that lead to "growth in connection" with supportive outcomes called the "five good things: zest, empowered action, increased knowledge, increased self-worth, and a desire for more connection."[8] Meanwhile, at the Center for Gender in Organizations at Simmons College, Joyce Fletcher, Roy Jacques, and their colleagues are analyzing "relational practice," the relational skills that women use to accomplish organizational goals.[9]

On the basis of this theory and research, some writers conclude that women leaders have a "female advantage," in Sally Helgeson's words, a preference for using different relational skills than men.[10] As applied to women in management, however, the female advantage hypothesis has been notoriously difficult to prove.[11] For Jean Baker Miller, the practical importance of developmental research is not to contrast women and men but to reveal the hidden potential in us all:

> *What we find when we study women are parts of the total human potential that have not been fully seen, recognized, or valued. These are parts that have not therefore flourished, and perhaps they are precisely the ingredients that we must bring into action in the conduct of all human affairs.*[12]

Unfortunately, even studies of women miss "parts of the total human potential" when researchers fail to study women from various racial, ethnic, and socioeconomic groups.[13] Much of the research on women in management has focused on white women from relatively privileged socioeconomic backgrounds, while much of the research on African American, Mexican American, and Puerto Rican women has dealt with low-income women, not college-educated women in professional positions. According to Karin Elliott Brown, Tyan Parker-Dominguez, and Marcia Sorey, "research is almost silent in its exploration of life stress, social support and well-being among African American women across social–economic status."[14] Furthermore, the experiences of African American women leaders do not always compare to the experiences of women leaders from other racial or ethnic groups of color.[15] International feminists criticize U.S. researchers for generalizations about women leaders of color, such as their assumptions that women of color come from families that are poor.[16]

Whatever their racial, ethnic, or socioeconomic backgrounds, women in our focus groups used their relational skills to resist prejudice and discrimination by building alternative systems of support. Lacking traditional mentors, they entered into mutually supportive relationships with other women leaders who were their peers. Peer mentors enjoyed "growth in connection," in Miller and Stiver's words, as they advanced together throughout their careers. As in the Girl Scout song, the women leaders learned to "make new friends and keep the old."[17] When they did not have peers from their own ethnic communities, they formed coalitions with other ethnic groups. A Puerto Rican woman leader joined African American educational and professional groups, making "the translation from the African American experience to the Latino experience."

Nearly all the women in our focus groups identified other women as significant sources of support. Excluded from "old boys' networks," they formed formal and informal networks with other women who shared their goals. A white woman leader remembered being shunned by male colleagues in an association of social work deans: "When I came in, there were very few women, and we bonded together." An African American woman leader said, "I can't imagine how women make it without strong women friends." Another white woman leader agreed:

> *In my early career, I was usually the only woman in the group or one of two. Initially, I just lived with it. Then I sought out other women and participated in a women's network, which I have remained with for over 20 years. As time went on, I was more aware of the need for the company of other women and was more aggressive in seeking them out.*

In a study of social support among 73 college-educated African American women, social work researchers Elliott Brown and her colleagues discovered the importance of women's friendships with other women. In response to Brown's survey, African American women ranked female friends as their most helpful source of social support and mothers as their second most helpful source of support.[18] These findings were consistent with the experiences of the women in our focus groups from various racial, ethnic, and socioeconomic backgrounds.

In professional development, as in psychological development, researchers may find new patterns or possibilities when they study the experiences of women from diverse racial, ethnic, and socioeconomic groups. According to literary scholar Carolyn Heilbrun, biographers often miss the significance of women's friendships with other women.[19] The same criticism may apply to organizational researchers who overlook women friends and informal women's networks as sources of support to women in leadership positions.[20]

Much management literature is based on the career patterns of the CEOs of large corporations, who are predominantly white men. Reflecting the culture of the corporate world, researchers present social support from an individualistic point-of-view, seeing mentors as the key to corporate success.[21] Management literature encourages women to follow the examples of men by seeking mentors in senior management, preferably mentors with racial and ethnic backgrounds similar to the women's own.[22] According to this advice, women managers, like men before them, will advance with the help of a few individuals who provide them with social, emotional, and instrumental support.

Women in our focus groups rarely found such mentors (see chapter 3).[23] They understood social support from a systems perspective rather than from an individualistic point-of-view. They did not rely on a few individuals for all the help that they might need but cultivated ever-expanding networks of social support, and they used this strategy, born of necessity, throughout their careers.

By the time of the focus group discussions, women had reached parity with men as leaders in many human services organizations. Today, according to the women leaders, nearly 50 percent of Urban League chapters are directed by women and nearly 50 percent of social work schools are led by women deans.[24] Nonetheless, the women leaders introduced younger women to their informal women's networks and recommended that they cultivate their own "circles of supportive women friends." As a white woman leader advised, "Find a supportive network of women friends, and keep track of them with care."

In addition to peer mentors and informal women's networks, women in our focus groups participated actively in formal professional associations such as the American Association of State Colleges and Universities, the Association of Black Social Workers, the Association of Baccalaureate Social Work Program Directors, the Council on Social Work Education, the National

Association of Deans and Directors, and NASW. Professional associations provided resources for enriching knowledge and skills, learning about changes and trends in the professional environment, forming new alliances and friendships, and organizing social and political action.

The women leaders founded formal and informal networks and constituency groups within their professional associations. Some women leaders joined "communities of practice," where they explored "shared expertise and passion for a joint enterprise," such as applying new technologies in human services.[25] Nearly all the women leaders participated in women's networks within their professional associations and formed affinity groups for colleagues from similar racial or ethnic backgrounds; for lesbian, gay, bisexual, or transgender colleagues; or for colleagues with disabilities.

Organizational researchers have documented the usefulness of women's networks and ethnic affinity groups in corporate settings as resources for professional development, mutual aid, and social action.[26] Catalyst identified women's networks and ethnic affinity groups as "best practices" for promoting equity and reducing discrimination in corporations.[27] In professional associations, as in corporations, these groups sponsor educational programs related to cultural competence and diversity, provide community service, and hold social events. In addition, they document discriminatory practices, propose alternatives, and advocate for change in the association, in human services organizations, and in the larger political arena.[28] For example, Latino/Latina social workers within the Connecticut state chapter of NASW organized the Latino/Latina Social Workers Network, which, among other activities, advocates to improve recruitment and retention of Latino/Latina students in local colleges and universities.

Women in our focus groups developed their capacities and skills as leaders by cultivating networks of support. In their relationships with families, friends, communities, and organizations, particularly in "strong relationships with women," they learned to believe in themselves, to resist prejudice and discrimination, and to hold on to their values and goals. As they advanced in their careers, they continued to give and receive support in relationships with peer mentors, formal and informal networks, and professional associations; and they reached out to younger women as role models and mentors. The women leaders put remarkable energy into their relationships. As a Mexican American woman leader explained, "I have been taught that relationships are the most important things in life."

ॐॐॐ

Summing Up Chapter 5:
Themes from the Focus Groups

- Women in our focus groups formed expansive networks of social support.
- They did not distinguish between personal and professional relationships as resources in their careers.
- They entered new relationships while sustaining earlier ties with families, friends, communities, and organizations.
- They resisted prejudice and discrimination by building alternative support systems.
- Lacking traditional mentors, they became peer mentors.
- Working in solo status, they entered multicultural coalitions.
- They balanced many commitments.
- Many felt supported by their husbands or partners.
- Nearly all the women leaders relied on women friends.
- They were active in professional associations, where they founded women's networks and ethnic affinity groups.
- They reached out to younger women as role models and mentors.

ॐॐॐ

Action Steps

What Do You Think?

Where do you turn for support in your education and your career? List all your sources of emotional and practical help, such as family, friends, teachers, mentors, classmates, colleagues, groups, helping professionals, spiritual relationships, and others. Consider relationships from childhood and relationships with people you have recently met. How have you expanded your support networks in the past? Where can you find new sources of support?

What Can You Do?

Identify one professional network or community group, and learn how to join it. This may be a college club, a community book club or discussion group, a parent–teacher organization, a virtual network, or a professional association. Participate in one network or group meeting or activity and exchange phone numbers or e-mail addresses with a member of the group. Alternatively, if you already are active in a professional network, bring a newcomer to a meeting and introduce her to your colleagues and friends.

Where Can You Read More about Sources of Support?

Catalyst. (1999a). *Creating women's networks: A how-to guide for women and companies*. San Francisco: Jossey-Bass.

Fletcher, Joyce K. (1999b). *Disappearing acts: Gender, power, and relational practice at work*. Boston: MIT Press.

❧

Part II

Leading from an Inclusive Perspective

Chapter 6

❧

How Do You
Change the World?

"As a collective, we are a relentless force for change."

SOUTH ASIAN WOMEN LEADERS

Women in our focus groups lived their values, valued their relationships, and pursued their visions of diverse, equitable, and effective human services. As leaders and agents of change, they understood integrity as the basis of power and power as the ability "to make a difference" to other people.

❧ ❧ ❧

Notes from Karen's Diary:
Power

Power is not derived from a position or a single act or accomplishment. Power lies in qualities of personal spirit and constancy of behavior, in working with rather than managing people. When I think of powerful people, I think of people who recognize their own limitations; who appreciate the

99

resources, strengths, and skills of others; who touch and affirm others; and who believe in a future.

My power is derived from a set of principles that places people and relationships first, that does not value "me first," that realizes that any organization is only the sum of the people that comprise it. Placing people first means listening actively to positions that are different from my own, listening to as many people as possible from as many perspectives as possible, particularly those people who will be affected by the decisions being discussed. Listening before making decisions can be slow and tedious. Delegating real responsibility and authority can be frightening. But the result is power, power found in the loyalty of organizational members, in the reciprocity of people who feel valued, in the productivity and good will of people who are willing to go the extra mile.

A commitment to people requires connecting to people. We must not permit our lives to become so busy, so goal directed or even so family oriented that we miss the connections, the ways and times for bringing the parts of our lives together. We are constantly admonished to keep personal life separate from work, not to bring personal problems to the workplace or workplace issues to our homes, but I find it impossible to maintain this separation. I am not, mind you, trying to pry into colleagues' private lives, but when working long hours side by side, promoting teamwork and shared vision, it is important to have some understanding, some caring, in relationships at work. In this "customer-oriented" society, we can't expect employees to treat clients better than they feel treated themselves. If we want to serve clients better, then we need to figure out better ways to treat the service providers, to create a good organizational climate, and to promote healthy interactions that help people grow.

Although connecting to the whole person is a principled and humane approach to leadership, connecting to or bridging ideas is the path toward excellence and creativity. We can't bridge ideas, learn something new, see something differently, if we only listen to ourselves or see what we've always seen. If I do all the talking, I really can't understand how others feel or what they think, and they can't feel included in my vision or my plan. People need first to feel valued and safe to talk freely. Then they need to be listened to.

So I do more listening than talking, and when I listen, I create power. I have often been complimented for being a good listener. I work at listening; I actively listen. Sometimes it's hard to listen because I want to concentrate on what I want to say and how I want to say it. Sometimes it's hard to listen because I don't agree, don't like what someone is saying. But I work at making myself open to ideas, not being threatened by a position different from mine, not dismissing the words if I don't like the body language or the tone of voice. And I know that I like to be listened to in that way. I appreciate it when the people I am talking to nod, smile, and look thoughtful, when they verbally acknowledge what I've said and build on it. I try to do that for others in turn.

Our society might have been founded on an individualistic paradigm, fiercely competitive, marketplace driven, but life is really not about that. Life is about collaboration, making things happen in families, in work, in community, through joint efforts. Tasks might be accomplished individually, but reaching to create a new goal requires the best parts of many people working together. And that collaboration builds a power base as well, bringing people together around common ideas, principles, and goals rather than building competing factions. "We" is much more powerful than "I."

Optimism is another source of power because it is an essential part of vision. Pursuit of the new idea, of the seemingly impossible, takes an optimistic worldview. People have asked me over the years how it is that I see a different world, a different version of what they see. My answer is that I work at that optimism. Optimism helps me focus not on how much I know, but on how much I can learn; not on whether a person is smart, but on how this person is smart. It focuses not on how wrong things are, but how good they have been, how much better they might become. Sometimes I believe I'm the only one who really likes my job. When people ask me, "How is it going?" I respond 90 percent of the time with "I really enjoy what I'm doing; the people I work with are great; there are a lot of exciting opportunities ahead." There is power in the positives.

So for me, commitment, connection, collaboration, and optimism are the bases of power. Committing to sound principles and holding them constant set the course; connecting to people and ideas different from my own nurtures creativity. That connection allows for collaboration, and optimism shines the light for the future.

꒒꒒꒒

Just as Karen found power in commitment, connection, collaboration, and optimism, so women in our focus groups led from an inclusive perspective based on social responsibility, participatory decision making, and an appreciation for diversity.

Responding to obstacles with perseverance and hope, they were optimists who learned to fit into human services organizations while also trying to change them. In the words of researchers Deborah Meyerson and Maureen Scully, the women leaders were "tempered radicals." They advanced their causes along with their careers, pursuing changes "to make the workplace more equitable and inclusive."[1]

They had no illusions about the progress that they had made. As a white woman leader said, "In spite of my achievements, I do not believe that I have overcome these barriers, because the next person coming after me will have to deal with them." The women in our focus groups were not fooled by illusions of inclusion, approaches to "diversity management" that leave discriminatory barriers in place. In particular, they saw through three illusions—the illusion of numbers, the illusion of color blindness, and the illusion of marginality—as false beliefs and barriers to social change (Table 6-1).

Table 6-1
Illusions of Inclusion in Human Services Organizations

	Illustion of Numbers	Illustion of Color Blindness	Illusion of Marginality
Illusion	Change is by numbers alone	Everyone is the same	Diversity is at the margins
Reality	Exclude diversity Power differentials	Deny diversity Differential expectations	Isolate diversity Differential opportunities
Target of Change	Individuals	Formal policies	Deep structure

The Illusion of Numbers

As the first women or the first women from their racial or ethnic groups to lead their organizations, women in our focus groups saw through the illusion of numbers, the illusion that change happens by numbers alone. Refusing to be tokens, they understood that "being there" was not enough. They had to work for change.

Some writers cling to the illusion of numbers, the belief that organizational and professional cultures fundamentally change when more women and more people of color move into professional positions. In an interview with *The New York Times*, psychologist Carol Gilligan predicted a sea change in the legal profession when, in 2001, 50 percent of the students entering law schools were women.[2] The legal culture will become less competitive, less adversarial, more nurturing and humane, Gilligan claimed, but the evidence is not convincing. Professional schools that were once predominantly male, such as law schools, medical schools, and business schools, have admitted high proportions of women for many years, with little resulting difference in the leadership of those professions or in the professional values and norms.

Certainly, there is power in numbers. Women in our focus groups testified to the stress of working in solo status or being the firsts in their fields.[3] As compared with previous generations, the many women who are studying law, medicine, and business today enjoy unprecedented, though not unqualified, social acceptance and peer support. They can look up to women who are public figures in their professions, and they can follow the adventures of fictional women lawyers, judges, and doctors on TV.[4] Whether their professions have been predominantly male or female, however, women and professionals of color have not advanced into senior leadership positions in proportion to their numbers.

According to researchers Robin Ely and David Thomas, "Increasing the numbers of traditionally underrepresented groups without altering power relations between dominants and subdominants is unlikely to improve the position of those groups substantially."[5] In other words, successful women learn to play the game.[6] As a result, shifts in professional demographics do not necessarily change the "power positions" of groups or the policies and practices that favor the groups in power.

Power relations occur in nature, just as they occur in organizations, according to what biologists call the "law of the retarding lead." The dominant species is the last to adapt to changes in the natural environment, and so it is with people and organizations in power.[7] In their study of the power elite—leaders in U.S. corporations, government, and the military—sociologists Richard Zweigenhaft and William Domhoff made the strange discovery that diversity has reinforced the status quo: "The power elite has been strengthened because diversity has been achieved primarily by the selection of women and minorities who share the prevailing perspectives and values of those already in power."[8] As an example, George W. Bush has presided over a more diverse administration than any previous Republican president, but his policies have not improved the social and economic positions of women or low-income ethnic communities.

According to international researchers Aruna Rao, Stuart Rieky, and David Kelleher, most organizations are managed through "exclusionary power regimes" that "devalue participation and silence the voices that would bring . . . alternative perspectives and knowledge."[9] Hiring and promoting like-minded managers, "women and minorities who think like we do," in the words of one CEO, organizations miss the point of diversity, the opportunity to learn from and adapt to diverse worldviews.[10] Increasing the number of managers from underrepresented groups is a necessary, but insufficient, condition for organizational change.

The Illusion of Color Blindness

The illusion of numbers, the illusion that diversity is achieved through numbers alone, is closely related to the illusion of color blindness, the illusion that equity is achieved by treating everyone the same. Discriminatory practices hide behind the "Golden

Rule." As explained by organizational consultant Roosevelt Thomas, Jr., if the Golden Rule means treating your neighbor as *you* would like to be treated, then we need a Platinum Rule: treat your neighbor as *your neighbor* would like to be treated.[11] When organizations try to treat everyone the same, they treat everyone according to the preferences of the group in power. One size rarely fits all, and policies and practices that fit mainstream managers often put other groups at a disadvantage.[12]

Many color-blind policies and practices that appear neutral with respect to sex, race, or ethnicity have discriminatory effects. For example, public agencies and state licensing boards increasingly rely on standardized tests in hiring, promoting, and licensing professional human services providers. Applicants from some groups—older applicants, low-income applicants, applicants with English as a second language, and applicants from some racial and ethnic groups—have disproportionately lower scores on these examinations than younger, more affluent, native English-speaking applicants. The use of test scores as the sole criterion for hiring or promoting has a discriminatory effect because test scores have not been proved to predict performance on the job.[13]

In reality, organizations do not treat everyone the same. Participating in the pervasive prejudices of the wider society, organizations are, at best, selectively color blind. Some managers are influenced by sexual, racial, and ethnic stereotypes in assigning tasks and evaluating performance (see chapter 3).[14] Women are often assigned the essential "relational work" of organizations, according to organizational researcher Joyce Fletcher. They build teams, prepare for meetings, mediate disputes, and teach or train others.[15] Women in our focus groups found that in universities where most faculty are white, women faculty of color have disproportionate responsibilities for relational work, such as mentoring students from their racial or ethnic groups. In other predominantly white human services organizations, professional women of color are assigned relational work outside the organization, such as serving as ambassadors to ethnic communities. At the organization's request, they represent the organization on agency boards, interagency task forces, and community forums.

Unfortunately for the women, relational work is "invisible work," in Fletcher's words.[16] Supervisors are more likely to recognize relational work by men than relational work by women, but generally speaking, relational work "disappears" from view when supervisors evaluate job performances, distribute merit pay, or award promotions. Organizations recognize and reward products, singular achievements by individuals, rather than processes, the underlying collaborations that make such achievements possible.

✦✦✦

Notes from Karen's Diary: Rules of the Game

Toward the end of my first year as dean, I looked forward to members of my faculty coming up for promotion and tenure. Two of the faculty members, a Mexican American man and an African American woman, were the only persons of color applying for promotion, and neither had the research record to attain it.

I suspected that these faculty members had performed extraordinary service for the university or for the community, so I called them in, each separately, for interviews. My hunch proved to be true. The Mexican American man had started his employment as an assistant professor, but he then served for several years as assistant dean. I knew that as an administrator, he had far less time for research and writing than teaching faculty have. The African American woman had served on twice as many university committees as her assistant professor colleagues. She also had advised more students.

I decided to take a request to the provost that both
these faculty members be allowed more time to achieve
tenure. It seemed reasonable to me that if the university
had asked them to provide more service than other faculty, giving up their time for research, then the system could
pay them back with additional time.

The provost refused. "In promotion and tenure decisions, everyone must play by the same rules," he explained.
I pointed out that the university is not playing by the rules
when it assigns more work to some faculty than to others.
I repeatedly had to fight for these candidates. Eventually,
the provost agreed, but without ever seeing the systemic
inequities involved. "Karen," he told me, "you're just a bleed-
ing heart."

❧ ❧ ❧

Karen's faculty members did not know the rules, particularly
the informal rules of the game. Without mentors or networks to
guide them, they lacked good information for assessing opportunities, negotiating rewards, and deciding how or when to say
no. If he had had a mentor, the Mexican American professor
would have understood the risks in becoming assistant dean. He
might have tried to negotiate "stopping the tenure clock" or
postponing his research while serving in administration. If she
had had a professional network, the African American professor would have understood the risks of giving priority to university service over her research and writing. She would have known
that the need to "publish or perish" is an acceptable reason for
turning down committee assignments.

Invisible work goes to women and professionals of color who
lack alliances with people in power in the organization. By joining together, they can develop their own alliances with peer mentors and networks, discover information, and negotiate the
written and unwritten rules of the game.

The Illusion of Marginality

Illusions of inclusion are dangerous to organizations. They are blinds to diversity, concealing the depth and breadth of environmental change. Organizations with the illusion of numbers exclude or suppress different perspectives and points of view. Organizations with the illusion of color blindness deny that differences exist. Organizations with the illusion of marginality isolate differences, adapting as little as possible to changes in the workforce and in client communities.

The illusion of marginality is the illusion that diversity exists on the margins of society. Diversity, in this view, refers to "minority groups" and "special populations," people from different backgrounds and different perspectives than the majority mainstream or the predominant groups in power. To accommodate diversity in the workforce, organizations with the illusion of marginality develop separate career tracks for women and professionals of color, who in turn provide services to ethnic communities. Alternative career tracks meet the needs of some individuals but often have discriminatory effects. When organizations steer some groups into positions with lower compensation or fewer advancement opportunities than other groups have, then alternative career tracks contribute to occupational segregation.

The "mommy track" may be the most famous example. Alternative career tracks for professional women with children allow women to work fewer or more flexible hours than usual in exchange for lower pay and limited possibilities for advancement. With the mommy track, organizations treat a central issue for workers as a marginal issue for women, mistaking general for special needs. According to recent research, most women and men in the U.S. workforce balance work with family and community responsibilities, and most workers want more flexibility and control over their time. In a study of 7,500 working Americans, Harvard researcher Jody Heymann found that nearly all workers, both women and men, have caregiving responsibilities in families and communities, including child care, eldercare,

care for spouses or partners, and care for neighbors and unre-
lated adults.[17]

Alternative career tracks are stopgap measures in place of more
fundamental structural and cultural organizational change. When
a white woman leader in our focus groups, a university dean,
realized the general importance of family to her faculty and staff,
she worked with them to create a "family-friendly" work environment for all:

> *I have tried to create an atmosphere in the school where*
> *family comes first. I have a male associate director*
> *who has lunch with his recently widowed mother ev-*
> *ery Friday and takes her to her hair appointment. If a*
> *conflicting meeting comes up that can be changed, we*
> *change it. If a meeting comes up that can't be changed,*
> *then I cover for him, just as he covers for me if my son*
> *is presenting a school project and wants me to be there.*
> *Initially, I felt as if I had to prove that I could still*
> *work hard if I had young children and that work*
> *should come first. Then I began to notice that every*
> *one of our faculty and staff has some sort of family*
> *responsibilities with parents or kids or spouses or part-*
> *ners and that allowing time for this makes our work*
> *together more productive.*

Some alternative career paths, such as the mommy track, are
established through formal policy, while others arise from informal practice. Ethnic niche career tracks result from the informal
practice of assigning professional positions because of sex or
race. Human services organizations may have satellite offices or
outreach centers in low-income, ethnic communities. When
women managers or managers of color are routinely assigned to
the satellite office rather than to the main office, an ethnic niche
career track is made.[18] Supervisors sometimes make sex-based
or race-based assignments without discriminatory intent. They
do not see the stereotypes in their decisions. Women sometimes
move unknowingly onto ethnic niche career tracks. They accept

positions in ethnic communities as opportunities to serve the communities well. When they apply for promotions, however, the doors to the main office are closed to them.

In organizations with the illusion of marginality, ethnic niche experience is considered marginal experience with little relevance to the rest of the organization. Knowledge related to women or ethnic minority communities is seen as specialized knowledge, applicable only to those groups. Knowledge related to majority or mainstream groups is seen as general knowledge, applicable to all. As a result, organizations with the illusion of marginality fail to learn from their own diversity. Just as the seemingly special needs of professional women indicate general needs for family-friendly policies, so the culturally sensitive services provided to one ethnic community suggest possibilities for improving services to others.

South Asian women in our focus groups provided an example. The South Asian women leaders founded SNEHA, a community-based support network for Connecticut women of South Asian origin.[19] Drawing from their bicultural experience, these women leaders combined mainstream and culturally specific approaches to interpersonal helping. As described in the organizational brochure:

> SNEHA, Inc., is an organization for women of South Asian origin and their families. We operate on the basis of a unique extended family model, where we combine the trust, sympathy, affection, and respect characteristic of our aunts, elder sisters, and grandmothers, with the best of self-help networks prevailing in the U.S. We work at three levels for the empowerment of women: the society, the community, and individuals.
> - We work to change mainstream perceptions of new immigrants. . . .
> - Within our community, we provide a forum where women and men of all language groups, religions and generations . . . discuss issues of pan-ethnic interest. . . .

- At the heart of our activities is our service for individual empowerment. We reach out to all women seeking sympathetic and confidential support on matters that cause them anxiety. We serve as empathic listeners and provide information and referral on medical, legal and social services available locally, nationally and internationally.
- As SNEHA members, we serve unobtrusively, with respect and affection towards our community. As a collective, we are a relentless force of change of all circumstances which have a detrimental effect on our lives.[20]

For mainstream social workers, some of this language sounds familiar. Schooled in systems theory and empowerment practice, social workers effect change at many levels in the relationships between individuals and their environments.[21] However, social workers rarely compare their relationships with clients to the relationships of aunts or grandmothers. They are taught to distinguish between professional and personal roles. In planning SNEHA, the South Asian women leaders reached out to women who would rather turn to family than to strangers for help. The extended family model stands in for extended family networks in India, allowing immigrant women to find and build community as they adapt to their new home.

When human services organizations fail to learn from and adapt to the communities that they serve, professional concepts such as respecting boundaries or avoiding dual relationships become cultural barriers to clients. With culturally sensitive approaches like the extended family model, organizations reach out to ethnic and immigrant communities, including white ethnic communities. An approach designed for one group may also appeal to others. As organizations see beyond the illusion of marginality, they integrate rather than segregate ethnic experience, ending separate career tracks on the ethnic niche. Women managers with culturally specific knowledge and experience are welcomed to mainstream positions where they can disseminate cultural knowledge throughout the organization's programs and services.

The illusion of marginality obscures the importance of diversity and equity for providing effective human services. When diversity and equity are seen as marginal, as separate and apart from organizational effectiveness, then discriminatory policies and practices are unlikely to end. When diversity and equity are seen as integral to all other goals of an organization—its mission, its excellence, and its survival—then the organization can change its exclusionary approach to power.

Windows to Change

Illusions of inclusion are false beliefs that provide opportunities for change. By joining together, women and men from various racial and ethnic groups, including managers, service providers, communities, and clients, can identify the discriminatory practices and disparate effects that they have experienced in human services organizations. In organizations with the illusion of numbers, women and people of color can document that change is not, in fact, happening by numbers alone. Recruitment of women managers may be high, but retention remains low. More women and women of color may be entering management, but relatively few are advancing into senior leadership positions. Services to culturally diverse clients and communities are no better than before.

As the illusion of numbers fades, organizations may try individualistic approaches to change. Researchers at the Center for Gender in Organizations call these approaches "fixing the woman."[22] "Fix-the-woman" approaches socialize underrepresented groups into the organization, providing them with skills that they missed by living or working outside the mainstream. Management training for women, minority fellows programs, even test preparation courses are all designed to prepare individuals to meet organizational norms. Fix-the-woman approaches do not directly change the organization. Individuals bear responsibility for change.

In organizations with the illusion of color blindness, women and people of color can expose the illusion that everyone is treated the same. They can identify and document formal policies and practices that give some groups advantages over others. Evidence of discriminatory effects is useful in negotiating with the organization to end such practices and to remedy the effects of past discrimination. In colleges and universities, faculty have documented sex-based salary differentials and have negotiated for salary scales that would bring women to parity. When the illusion of color blindness is revealed, organizations may "level the playing field" by changing the formal policies and practices that have had disparate effects on women and other groups.[23] "Leveling the playing field" affects formal rules of the game, leaving informal practices in place.

Of all the illusions of inclusion, the illusion of marginality is the least visible to those associated with an organization. Like a one-way mirror, the illusion of marginality reflects the power relations and conflicts, prejudices, and stereotypes of the wider society. Women and people from various racial and ethnic groups soon learn the difference between marginal acceptance and meaningful inclusion. They see patterns of exclusion, differential opportunity structures that open different doors to different groups, but they have difficulty locating the policies or practices at fault. As described by a Puerto Rican woman leader, "Those barriers are hidden under the surface. Sometimes you're not aware of them . . . but the opportunity somehow is not there for you."

Deep Structure

On the surface, a woman's experience in an organization, her feelings of inclusion or exclusion, of belonging or isolation, appear to be an individual's subjective response. A woman's success, accomplishments, and setbacks look like the results of her own efforts, abilities, and choices. Under the surface, however, the organization is providing some groups with different alliances and networks, as well as resources and information, than other groups have. These activities, hidden from view, are what

Aruna Rao and her colleagues call the "deep structure" of organizations (see chapter 3). According to Rao, all organizations have a deep structure, an "unquestioned, normal way of working."[24] Formal and informal policies, practices, processes, and symbols "combine to make inequality not only an important part of a wide variety of interactions but also very difficult to see."[25]

Individual experiences in an organization are windows to the deep structure. To see beyond individual experience, women and people from various racial and ethnic groups can explore their experiences together, examining their places in the organization, from day-to-day relationships to friendships that extend beyond work. They can identify feelings of comfort and discomfort in meeting rooms and in lunchrooms, hallway conversations and social events, and they can consider their place in decision making during routine operations and extraordinary circumstances.[26] They also can review the organization's traditions, stories, and symbols. Do pictures in the organizational literature show white men in professional positions but no women professionals or professionals of color? Do they show white professionals helping clients of color but no professionals of color helping white clients? Are some groups of workers or clients never shown at all?

When various groups in the organization search for the deep structure, they reveal its illusions of inclusion, its false hopes and false beliefs about itself. Identifying prejudices and stereotypes that perpetuate discrimination, they locate formal and informal decision-making processes that have discriminatory effects.

Unfortunately, however, groups that experience discrimination do not always join together in social action. Some underrepresented groups approach other groups as rivals. Aware of particular prejudices against themselves and influenced by prejudices against others, they have a sense of "competing oppressions." The needs of one's own group take priority over the needs of others. As explained by researcher Deborah Merrill-Sands and her colleagues, "Raising one aspect of equity raises others. This does not create a natural alliance but creates an opportunity for a planned alliance."[27] Inclusive leaders use their relationships with diverse communities to build connections among groups, planning alliances through such collaborative activities as participatory action research.[28]

Participatory Action Research

People in an organization search for deep structure through participatory action research. As action researchers, they look for policies or practices that discriminate against particular groups of human services providers, clients, or communities. Social values are the bedrock of deep structure in human services organizations, and competing groups often come together around their commitment to the clients and communities that they serve.

Catalyst recommends participatory action research as the means to organizing women's networks and ethnic affinity groups.[29] As women respond to surveys, interviews, and focus group discussions about their experiences in the organization, they become interested in joining together for information and support. Researchers Deborah Meyerson and Joyce Fletcher advise women to focus on "small wins" when they enter into action research. Participants choose a few discrete targets for change, take experimental steps in changing them, and evaluate the results.[30] Community developers also take incremental steps to social change, using participatory action research in an educational process called praxis: research, action, reflection, research.[31]

In each case, participatory action research starts social action with social learning. Finding a chink in the deep structure of organizations, research participants generate energy for change. One small change leads to other changes large and small, and as systems theorists have shown, local activities have global effects. A report by women faculty at the Massachusetts Institute of Technology (MIT) provides a vivid example. When faculty researched sexual discrimination in the MIT School of Science, their findings, intended as an internal report, shook illusions of inclusion in research universities throughout the United States.

A Virtuous Circle

In the 1990s, the percentage of women science students was rising in U.S. graduate schools, but the percentage of women scientists on the faculty of research universities was hardly rising at all. Most research universities denied or dismissed complaints of sexual discrimination by women scientists. In contrast, Charles M. Vest, the president of MIT, responded seriously to women's concerns.[32] He supported Professors Nancy Hopkins, Lotte Bailyn, and Lorna Gibson in forming a research committee to analyze the experiences of women faculty in the School of Science. The committee included not only the women scientists, but also influential and skeptical male faculty. As the committee of scientists gathered extensive quantitative data and as evidence of discrimination mounted, the men on the committee joined the women's cause.

The committee's report, issued in 1999, documented that tenured women faculty received fewer resources for research and lower salaries than men with the same qualifications.[33] More significant, women were consistently excluded from decision-making roles in their departments. Faced with comprehensive data, President Vest publicly acknowledged that MIT had discriminated against women. The story made the national news. When women scientists at other research universities presented evidence of sexual discrimination, it was far more difficult to ignore them.

In 2001, the president of MIT met with the presidents of eight other top research universities, and they signed a pledge "to promote the more equitable treatment of female faculty members in science and engineering, and to consider potentially significant changes in university policies to accomplish that goal."[34] They agreed to analyze salaries and resources of women scientists at their institutions, to diversify faculty, and to consider policies related to work–family balance.

It is a long way to equity for women scientists, particularly women scientists of color.[35] Even so, we can celebrate MIT's "small win." Professor Nancy Hopkins and her colleagues used capacities for social action, skills for social learning, and social justice values to promote diversity and equity in their organization. With support from Vest and others in senior leadership positions, they turned a vicious cycle of discrimination into a virtuous circle of change.

ॐॐॐ

Summing Up Chapter 6

- Illusions of inclusion—the illusion of numbers, the illusion of color blindness, and the illusion of marginality—are approaches to diversity that perpetuate discrimination in human services organizations.
- Illusions of inclusion prevent organizations from responding to widespread changes in the environment, such as workforce needs for work–family balance and community needs for culturally sensitive services.
- Organizations have deep structures: traditions, assumptions, and decision-making processes that effectively exclude some groups from information, resources, and opportunities.
- People are so accustomed to discriminatory processes that they may not be aware of possibilities for changing them.
- Organizations end discriminatory practices only when they appreciate diversity and equity as integral to other organizational goals.
- Targets of organizational change may be individuals, formal policies and practices, and informal processes in the deep structure of organizations.
- Women can organize to change discriminatory practices through participatory action research.

ॐॐॐ

Action Steps

What Do You Think?

Choose an organization you know well. How well does the organizational mission—its formal values and goals—reflect the organizational reality? Consider policies, programs and services, assumptions and beliefs, and the ways people treat each other. How is the deep structure of your organization—the unspoken values, expectations, and beliefs—revealed in an organizational publication, photograph, ceremony, or story? What illusions of inclusion do you find?

What Can You Do?

Identify two or three women in an educational or professional position similar to yours. They may be classmates in school, colleagues in the workplace, or members of a professional network or community group (see "What Can You Do?" in chapter 5). Make a date to talk about the women's goals, barriers, and resources for meeting them. What barriers and resources do the women have in common? What additional resources do they need? How would you find out whether other women in the organization or group have similar needs? Gathering such information is the first step in participatory action research.

Where Can You Read More about
Ending Discrimination in Organizations?

Meyerson, Deborah E. (2001). *Tempered radicals: How people use difference to inspire change at work*. Cambridge, MA: Harvard Business School Press.

Rao, Aruna; Rieky, Stuart; & Kelleher, David. (1999). *Gender at work: Organizational change for equity*. West Hartford, CT: Kumarian Press.

Chapter 7

❧

How Are You Leading Human Services?

"Lead with humor, lead with grace, open doors, and be true to yourself."

WOMEN LEADERS FOCUS GROUP

For women in our focus groups, cultivating relationships was a way of leading and a way of life. Caring for families, communities, and organizations from day to day, they attended to their many relationships in the process of leading human services organizations, and the process of leadership was as important to them as the results. In this sense, their work was consistent with "women's ways of leading" in corporate management, as described by Judith Rosener and other writers.[1] As change agents and leaders, however, the women in our focus groups transcended gender roles. Guided by personal, cultural, and professional values and goals, they promoted diversity and equity in their organizations, and they strengthened the potential of their organizations to lead wider social change.

Building Community

The process of social change begins with building community, and as Karen found, the process of building community begins at home. If a human services organization is to engage in participatory decision making, then participants in the organization need to express organizational values and goals in the ways that they work together from day to day.

ﾞﾞﾞ

Notes from Karen's Diary:
Change

I sometimes have started things that have become much larger organizational changes than I planned them to be. In fact, if I had thought at times that I was trying to change an entire organization, I might have been more reluctant to take it on.

When I became dean at the School of Social Work, the internal climate was unpleasant and dysfunctional. Interactions among faculty members or between faculty members and staff were less than civil. People in faculty meetings were not listening to each other; they were interrupting and screaming at each other! Ideas weren't being built on or shared.

I knew when I took the position that the school faced major challenges, but with the internal climate as it was, there was no opportunity for consensus building to do this work. I came to realize that returning civility to the workplace would be an important underpinning to getting anyplace else.

For me, the question was, How do I begin that kind of change? You don't just write governance policies of "Thou shall be civil!" In effect, I began to do and say just that. At large meetings, I began telling people that they were out of order when their language was abusive or when they interrupted colleagues. I purposively walked out of meetings at times when I felt that I couldn't gain the control I needed to bring about civility. That had never happened before in faculty meetings, but I knew that I couldn't be the only standard-bearer for civility. If there weren't other faculty willing to speak up and share their concerns about how we interacted as colleagues, then no amount of leadership or control was going to make that difference.

It was a change that came, and at first, it came as lots of changes. We just didn't allow people to be abusive with one another, and we allowed people to finish sentences and thoughts. We rotated through the faculty who wanted to speak and didn't allow all the speaking to be done by one or two people. As we saw from the civil rights movement, you can legislate behavior. From changed behavior, some people were moved to accept the underlying values we sought in the school. Others left the organization because they no longer could operate in the way they wanted to operate in a changed culture.

Change in organizational climate is always difficult, and many leaders ignore problems like lack of civility or trust. They see the other issues and think that they can tackle them and ignore the internal climate or the organizational culture. I have to be more or less continually monitoring the culture and going back to some of those basics, laying the foundation for larger organizational change.

When I became president of this university [the University of Houston–Victoria], I found a climate of nearly total distrust between faculty and administration. Once again, I realized that in order get any other change going, the organization needed some basis for renewed trust. If there is no trust in leadership, there are no easy answers except to say that you will be the model and that what you say is what you're going to do. If you are going to have governance work in the sunshine rather than behind closed doors, you just have to do it and do it repeatedly and do it continuously and tell people you are doing it. I never ask people to trust me. I just ask them to hear what I've said and watch what I do, and hopefully trust will build.

ॐ ॐ ॐ

Building Support

Inclusive leaders build community by cultivating relationships between and among various communities and groups. Women in our focus groups found personal and professional support in relationships sustained throughout their careers. From senior leadership positions, Karen similarly used her extensive relationships to gather information, to enhance resources, and to form political alliances for her organization.

ॐ ॐ ॐ

Notes from Karen's Diary: Support

When I was dean of the School of Social Work, the university began a capital campaign, and all the deans were asked to become fundraisers. We were given four or five hours of training. There were pieces on building relationships in the training, but many of my colleague deans understood building a relationship as "Let's go to a one-hour meeting and see if we can close the deal!"

The social work school was the first college to complete its fundraising goal and the only college to exceed its goal. Although our goal in dollars was not as high as that of some of the other colleges, the law school or the colleges of business and engineering, it was as much a stretch for us as their goals were for them. The other deans were continuously surprised that I had achieved it.

I was working from social work values and skills and from relationships that we already had built, and obviously I had a great deal of commitment to what I believed the school was about and the kind of projects that we were trying to fund. The social work school, and often that meant me, had relationships with people in the community. We had done community projects and done them well, and we had followed through with interns who worked in agencies and faculty who served on boards. As a school, we had a reputation of connection to the community. Taking some of those relationships to another level was much easier than the cold call, "close the deal" approach.

In a leadership position, you build good relationships wherever you are. People who have money are not always the most significant people in the community, and you really never know who is going to be a donor down the road. In the social work school, we had relationships with people that we never thought of as potential donors. They felt connected with the school, and when they came into money, they thought of us.

At my current university, there is a woman donor whose original intention was to give money to the neighboring community college. She got lost and arrived at our university by mistake, but since she was already there, she had a meeting with my development director and me. She got so excited by what we were doing that she wound up giving us the money! She tells the story now, and people find it very funny. I find it a good statement about how we were able to articulate a set of needs, whether it was student needs or community needs, that she found compelling. I believe also that she felt that the development director listened to her, and she found it meaningful to have direct access to me as the president.

Respectful relationships are reciprocal relationships, in fundraising as in everywhere else. It is easy to create fundraising goals by looking inward at the organization or talking to people inside the organization and asking, What do we need? Successful fundraising comes from talking to people outside of the organization and asking what they think the community needs or the region needs that the organization could provide. When people have been part of the discussion, they can be the people who, if not the donors themselves, go to prospective donors and help you to articulate those needs.

Building Strength

When women in our focus groups met barriers in their careers, they turned to networks and professional groups inside and outside their organizations. Alliances with community and professional leaders improved the women's standing in their own organizations and opened opportunities for advancement. From senior leadership positions, Karen similarly advocated for her university, strengthening her political standing with support from the community.

ॐॐॐ

Notes from Karen's Diary: Negotiation

When I think of negotiating, I first have a narrow focus, thinking of negotiating around an individual job and its salary or title. Yet, one really needs to think of negotiating more broadly in terms of goals, needs, and activities of an organization. When negotiation concerns larger organizational issues, it can take the form of grassroots organizing and political advocacy, and there is a whole set of very natural social work skills that come into play.

In my first year as president of a public university, one of the challenges that I didn't know I would face was that the new chancellor was not going to provide the monies, 10 million dollars, promised to the university by the previous administration. The monies had been promised in public, and legislators knew about them, community college officials knew about them, community leaders knew about them, but the chancellor was going to renege.

The chancellor was also my new boss. The difficulty, which is part of leadership, was, How could I be an effective team player in the larger system when that team was contradicting the goals of my own organization? I could not even get the issue to the Board of Regents for a discussion because the chancellor had to place the item on the agenda.

I struggled with that. If I couldn't get the topic to the board for discussion, the chancellor would just bury it, and the promised monies would never happen. It was major. It meant that we would not be able to purchase land or build buildings as planned. We would have to give back to the state the 10 million dollars that they had given to us because the university system had promised 10 million dollars in matching funds.

After many months of trying to figure out what to do, I invited the chancellor down to our campus for another event and then asked if he would talk with community leaders. We had produced a video of community leaders who were not able to be present. They talked about the importance of the university to the region. Then in the face-to-face meeting with other community leaders, the chancellor began to realize that the promise of funding was not something that I was fabricating. The community had heard it and expected it to happen. It began to force the issue so that there would be a negotiation because you can't have a negotiation if one party refuses even to bring the issue to the table. The issue eventually went into the legislative arena in the next legislative session. The legislators had also heard the system's commitment, and the university system came through with the funds.

کر کر کر

Building Coalitions

Sometimes human services organizations have larger goals than they can accomplish by themselves. As part of community building, leaders bring various organizations together in coalitions or partnerships. When organizations have similar values and goals, coalitions can expand organizational capacities and skills to effect social change.

ॐॐॐ

Notes from Karen's Diary:
Partnerships

Partnerships can increase the productivity of an organization and bring more resources to bear on a problem, but there is more to a partnership than realizing gains at the end. The process of creating and building a partnership provides other substantial gains in the organization's political viability, credibility, and support.

Partnerships are easier to establish and maintain when both parties come with some strengths or resources that the other party needs, such as intellectual capital or skills, and when both parties add something new and important rather than duplicating or competing with what already is being done. In that way, everybody feels that they are gaining through the partnership, not losing, because partnerships have hidden costs.

It takes considerable human resources to develop, nurture, and maintain partnerships consistently. The process piece has to be constantly watched, and the communication loops have to be attended to. People easily fall out of the loop of disseminating and receiving information. If communication erodes, then trust erodes, and the partnership becomes less effective.

There is no question in my mind that our partnerships have gone a long way to say to the community that we want to serve them, and we want to serve them in ways they help us identify. We will not sit here alone and determine what we believe is good for them. It's participatory, inclusive, and when we need help—whether it is help in writing to the legislature for funding or for passage of some bill, whether it is help in getting the message out—then we have partners that have already been involved.

えええ

Letting Education Achieve Dreams

In the Victoria region of South Texas, people are less likely to complete high school or college than people in nearly any other region of the United States. Among adults ages 25 or older, only 6 of 10 adults have a high school diploma, and only 1 in 10 has a bachelor's degree. Among Latinos/Latinas, the region's fastest-growing population group, only 4 of 10 adults have finished high school and only 1 in 50 has graduated from college.[2]

As president of the University of Houston–Victoria, Karen brought together diverse communities and organizations to work toward a radical social change: improving the educational attainment rates of all residents in the university's service area. Just as Karen is leading the university from an inclusive perspective, the university is leading the community, developing the community's capacities, skills, and values for social action, social learning, and social change.

えええ

Notes from Karen's Diary:
LEAD

Letting Education Achieve Dreams (LEAD) came initially out of our concern with attaining more diversity in our student population. We didn't know whether all student populations were getting the same information about college or whether they were getting the information that they needed.

We decided to talk with leaders in the African American, Asian, and Latino communities about our desire to attract and support a more diverse student population. We set up a series of roundtable discussions with community leaders. In addition to executives in the major organizations and corporations, we made sure we had leaders from religious groups, community associations, and the volunteer sectors in each community. We also brought in students from the community colleges and high schools.

Over and over again, people who came to the roundtables let us know that they could not recall ever having been brought to the university or asked for that kind of input before. There was an immediate positive response and a deep level of emotional commitment to working with us to help make a difference.

Up until those discussions, our university, like most universities nationally, had focused on the message that "college is affordable." That focus came out of the American Council on Education and its "College Is Possible" campaign. We learned from the African American and Latino/Latina community leaders that those were not the questions being asked. The problem is not that people are worried about college being unaffordable. The problem is that people aren't thinking of college at all! The community leaders helped us dramatically rethink what the message had to be, and it wasn't going to high schools and saying, "We can provide financial aid and scholarships." It was going into elementary schools and saying, "Here are careers, and here is the educational preparation for those careers."

When we stepped back from the roundtable discussions, we realized that this was huge. How do you wrap your arms around that kind of issue as a university and say that you are going to take it on? We invited back the original participants from the roundtable discussions, plus representatives from a number of other community groups, and we said, "This is what we are hearing and this is huge. Help us!"

The community participants affirmed that what we heard was what they believed. We decided to start an initiative called Letting Education Achieve Dreams, and the first goal would be to raise community awareness and community expectations for educational attainment. Even that is a huge goal when you are talking about a service region of half a million people spread over 200 square miles.

The message that we need to raise educational attainment levels is a difficult message for some constituents to hear. It has to be framed in a very diplomatic, very appropriate way so that you don't find yourself insulting people whose education has served them well but will not serve their children and their grandchildren well. This is a region based historically on agriculture and the petrochemical industry, where levels of education weren't high and didn't need to be high to have good jobs.

We took the risk, and we created large goals: raising community educational expectations, enhancing career awareness, enabling educational attainment, and promoting adult and parental involvement in education. We developed specific strategies to reach students from kindergarten through 12th grade, and we now are expanding our target populations from preschool children through all adults (Figure 7-1).

What we said from the beginning of the roundtable discussions is that our role is that of catalyst and coordinator. We are not here to duplicate or compete with any of the existing services or programs that are being done. We know mentoring is going on; there are just not enough mentoring programs or mentors. So in the area of mentoring, we are not providing mentors, but we are providing a curriculum that prepares mentors. We help corporations structure mentoring programs that will last over time, and we link schools with corporations or other organizations that want to provide mentoring. The Boys and Girls Club had volunteers who wanted to become mentors, and the Aransas/ Matagorda National Wildlife Refuge had rangers who wanted to become mentors, so we went there and helped them establish mentoring programs.

We developed talking points about the importance of getting more education, giving people information, and empowering them to go and talk to others. The community is now talking about educational attainment in so many places, in workplaces as well as at the Rotary Club, at the Chamber of Commerce, at service organizations. It has given us a great deal of visibility, press coverage, and television coverage.

We have been trying to be creative about age-specific content that engages children from a very young age in thinking about and seeing career opportunities. We have a puppet show that was developed by one of our graduates. Our students perform the puppet show when they go in and talk with second or third graders about careers and education. We have had fourth-, seventh-, and 10th-grade students come to campus, gearing the campus experience to their age groups.

We invested institutional resources for a year and went to the legislature for special line item funding, which we didn't get because that year the state fell short in revenues. However, when we asked people to write or call, we had an incredible outpouring of support, so we are very optimistic that we will find external funds.

Our long-term goal is to raise the educational attainment level in our region. That is the overarching goal of everything. We have some contractual partners, but beyond our formal contractual partners, we have a much larger

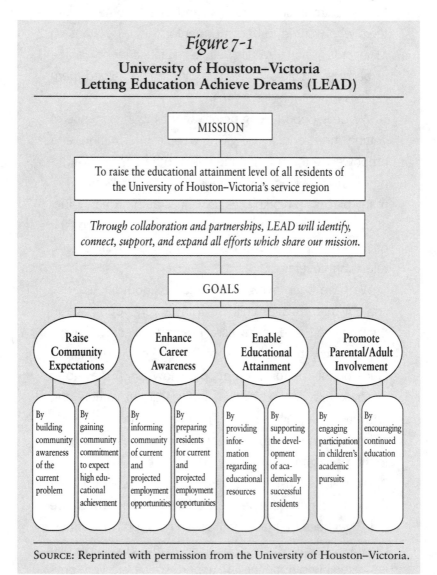

Figure 7-1

University of Houston–Victoria
Letting Education Achieve Dreams (LEAD)

MISSION

To raise the educational attainment level of all residents of the University of Houston–Victoria's service region

Through collaboration and partnerships, LEAD will identify, connect, support, and expand all efforts which share our mission.

GOALS

Raise Community Expectations	Enhance Career Awareness	Enable Educational Attainment	Promote Parental/Adult Involvement
By building community awareness of the current problem	By gaining community commitment to expect high educational achievement	By informing community of current and projected employment opportunities	By preparing residents for current and projected employment opportunities	By providing information regarding educational resources	By supporting the development of academically successful residents	By engaging participation in children's academic pursuits	By encouraging continued education

SOURCE: Reprinted with permission from the University of Houston–Victoria.

buy-in in terms of peoples' acknowledgment that this is a regional issue, a community issue. Everybody is in this together; everybody is concerned.

ॐॐॐ

Cultural Change

Testimony from participants in LEAD activities—public school students, teachers, principals, parents, and mentors—suggest the program's potential to effect cultural change locally, regionally, nationally, and within the university itself. A school principal noticed that students with mentors were showing academic improvements, some moving from near failure to the honor roll, but the mentoring program was also affecting students who did not themselves have mentors. They were beginning to find it socially acceptable and possible to do well in school.[3]

Middle-school students visiting the university campus were particularly impressed by the medical laboratory, the petrochemical processing plant, and riding on an elevator for the first time. They learned about differences between high school and college, such as opportunities to choose courses and to work while earning college credits. They were surprised to learn that college students who miss classes do not risk being taken to court. Entering the university buildings that some had passed all their lives, students sensed that they have a place in college. College is not for the rich alone.[4]

At national meetings with boards of governors of public universities, Karen is interested in shifting the dialogue from refining recruitment techniques to removing educational barriers to low-income ethnic communities. At the same time, the LEAD initiative has heightened awareness of the university mission within the university itself, raising questions about the meaning of education in the deep structure or the informal policies and practices of the organization.

Notes from Karen's Diary: Mission

Initiating a program like LEAD has internal as well as external effects. One of the positives has been talking about something in a variety of arenas, whether in staff council, faculty meetings, or other public forums that everybody in the organization can understand, see, and connect to. It has been a way of reinforcing our mission and saying to everybody, "We are higher education, and we are concerned about education for everybody."

Interestingly, from an employee perspective, we have not always been consistent in our message. The university has had a pool of scholarship money for our own staff to continue their educations. In one of my monthly coffees with staff, some staff members said, "You support us to go to school, you say education is important, but if we attain a degree that isn't absolutely required for our job, then there is no recognition for that."

That was a powerful statement, not a positive statement, but a powerful one! Now we are looking at a variety of ways to address that discrepancy. So the LEAD program has heightened our awareness as an organization of our mission and the need to be consistent in our message.

The Reality of Dreams

LEAD brings us full circle to the childhoods of our women leaders. What would a mentor have meant to Rosa, the young woman in foster care whose story introduced this book? Rosa dreamed of finishing high school, going to college, and becoming a social worker, but she had no consistent adults in her life to help her. What would a college visit or a puppet show about careers have meant for the women in our focus groups? They were told as children that "college would be a waste" or that "there are no jobs like that for colored girls."

Whatever the obstacles on their professional paths, the women in our focus groups found the motive, means, and opportunity to become leaders in human services. They had the motive of change agents, the desire to "make a positive difference" and "change the world," and it was as change agents that they began their human services careers. They took the means of explorers. Optimistic and confident in their ability to adapt to change, they reached out to new environments, technologies, and ideas. Finally, they created the opportunity of relationships, wide webs of relationships that embraced diverse communities and points-of-view. Multicultural in outlook and experience, they challenged prejudices and stereotypes wherever they found them. They were, in the words of a South Asian woman leader, "citizens of the world."

As change agents, explorers, and citizens of the world, women in our focus groups developed the capacities, skills, and values to lead from an inclusive perspective. They promoted diversity and equity as a means for improving the effectiveness of their organizations. As leaders in human services, however, the women's work was never done. They needed to reach out to new generations of women who, in the words of one woman leader, would carry on "the vision and reality of a just world for all persons."

This is why, when we asked them, the women leaders came to our focus groups. They came together as a community of mentors for women leaders of the future. They told stories about their families, their communities, and their first encounters with prejudice and discrimination. They described barriers they faced and choices they made as they advanced in their careers. They recalled the many people who gave them support, the "core values" that sustained them, and the meaning of their success. In the end, they offered these words of advice:

Hang in there! Have fun! Make a difference!

Expect to be successful and to be at the top of whatever it is you do. Expect to be a leader!

Don't let anybody tell you, "You can't." And know when to say no.

To the next generation, I would say look at your models, look at your parents, look at all the other mentoring people you have before you, and follow your dream. Whatever you want to do, do! Don't be locked into anything that you are pressured to do or feel that you must do because of somebody else's persuasion.

I suggest that prospective women leaders study the careers of women who came before them by observation, conversation, and reading biographies. Although times change, some situations do not. Pay attention to the attributes most rewarded in the organization or system, and expand knowledge in those areas. Build a strong support system, including women in like positions. E-mail makes these networks even more available than in prior times. Set your life goals, personal and professional, and focus on those. Do not allow yourself to be deflected from those goals unless or until you decide to change them. Remember to look behind you and assist other women in succeeding as well.

Go for what you want! There is never a good time to have a child or a good time to confront a controversial, important work issue. Make your time line for fulfilling your goals so that you never look back and say, "I wish I had done x, y, or z."

No matter what the situation, I would urge women to concentrate on doing good work, which is the best way of outperforming the competition. While there may be many helpful hints on how to get ahead, there is no substitute for competence. Hard work, confidence in one's ability, eagerness to learn, and a sense of humor are some of the ingredients of success. Always be true to yourself and your values, but don't take that self so seriously that it becomes a dominant factor in work or any aspect of life. All the women leaders I have known have consistently identified with something bigger than themselves and have never gotten bogged down in trivia. Also, they were obstinate. If there were obstacles, they persevered and fought, sometimes losing, but more often winning.

We just never know how we have touched others' lives. So my advice to women leaders is to be available to other young women who are struggling to reach their goals.

I would say, expand your vision of what "horizon" is. Sometimes we let ourselves accept the blinders that are put on us by the opportunities, the narrow opportunities that are right in front of us. So expand on these, look beyond them for what it is that would make you happy.

ↄↄↄ

Summing Up Chapter 7

- Organizations, like individuals, have values, capacities, and skills.
- Inclusive leaders develop organizational values, capacities, and skills to effect social change within and beyond their organizations.
- Participatory leadership requires consistent values and goals in the ways people work together from day to day.
- Inclusive leaders cultivate relationships with and among various communities and groups, using relationships to gather information, to enhance resources, and to form political alliances for their organizations.

- Organizations with similar values and goals can come together in coalitions, expanding organizational capacities and skills.
- Building and sustaining coalitions is an ongoing process that requires consistent communication within the organization as well as among participating groups.
- Just as individuals can provide inclusive leadership of organizations, organizations can lead communities from an inclusive perspective, developing community capacities, skills, and values for social change.

ぞぞぞ

Action Steps

What Do You Think?

What advice do you have for future women leaders? What comments do you have to the authors of this book?

What Can You Do?

Send suggestions and comments to lggardella@netscape.net.

Where Can You Read More about Leadership?

Freeman, Susan J. M., Bourque, Susan L., & Shelton, Christine M. (Eds.). (2001). *Women on power: Leadership redefined.* Boston: Northeastern University Press.

Wheatley, Margaret J. (1999). *Leadership and the new science: Discovering order in a chaotic world.* San Francisco: Berrett-Koehler.

Postscript to Educators

*"When one is accustomed to privilege,
equality seems like discrimination."*

<small>WOMEN LEADERS FOCUS GROUP</small>

"Women's experience is usually not what it has been said to be," in the words of Jean Baker Miller, and her observation applies to women leaders in human services.[1] Although social work is committed to culturally competent practice, our knowledge of women leaders has been based largely on the experiences of women managers in large corporations and on the perceptions of women from a narrow range of racial, ethnic, and socioeconomic backgrounds. Women leaders in human services, like the organizations they lead, may have different values and goals from women in corporate management, and women from different racial, ethnic, and socioeconomic groups may arrive at leadership along different paths.

The diversity among women leaders has posed challenges for organizational researchers. When women leaders are "firsts," when relatively few women leaders come from particular social groups, their experiences may be lost in large, aggregate studies. When, on the other hand, researchers try to "disaggregate data," looking closely at small groups of women leaders, they may be reluctant to generalize from a few women's experiences.[2]

Fortunately, we do not need to generalize to learn from diverse women leaders or to prepare women for leadership roles. Even when there are few women leaders from particular racial or ethnic groups, we can examine their experiences through qualitative research. Oral histories, narratives, and personal documents of individual women leaders enrich our understanding of women's careers.[3] Case studies of women leaders help us identify useful knowledge, skills, and values for leading human services organizations.

We chose to learn about culturally and socially diverse women leaders through the qualitative method of focus group research. Focus groups would suit the purposes of our book by allowing us to present women's experiences in their own words and from their own points of view. Through focus group discussions, women leaders would be able to reach out to readers, awakening their interest in becoming leaders and mentors themselves. Furthermore, women in the focus groups would reach out to one another, demonstrating the possibility of crossing racial, ethnic, and cultural differences to give and receive support.[4]

According to organizational researchers Ella Bell and Stella Nkomo, African American women and white women rarely come together as allies in corporate settings.[5] Even women from different racial and ethnic groups of color are separated by differences in cultural expectations, historical experiences, and communication styles.[6] For women leaders in human services, however, multicultural relationships are not only possible, they are essential to the work. Women leaders must use the knowledge, skills, and values of culturally competent practice to bridge cultural divides.[7]

To reflect the reality of human services, we tried to compose racially and ethnically heterogeneous focus groups whenever possible. According to social identity theory, heterogeneous focus groups would reveal more similarities than differences in the women leaders' experiences.[8] In ethnically homogeneous focus groups, the women leaders would be likely to explore their social identity, the meaning of their shared membership in a racial or ethnic group, while in ethnically heterogeneous focus groups, they would be likely to explore their personal identities, relating to one another as individuals with a common cause.[9] Two of our focus groups, including 18 women leaders, were heterogeneous. The third group, a focus group of five South Asian women leaders, was homogeneous in the sense that all the participants had emigrated from India. Although we perceived this focus group as homogeneous, the South Asian women leaders themselves perceived the group as culturally and ethnically diverse (Table P-1).

As white, straight researchers, we understood our limitations in learning about the experiences of women leaders from various racial, ethnic, and social backgrounds. We have not been the direct targets of racism and racial discrimination or of homophobia and heterosexist discrimination. When we invited women leaders to participate in focus groups, we would have limited credibility, particularly to women leaders who did not know us or our work.[10] Racially and ethnically diverse women leaders would participate in the focus groups if they agreed with the purpose of the research and if they trusted us to carry it out. Would we ask useful questions, listen carefully, and discern the meanings in women's responses? Would we include focus group participants who respect and value other women leaders and their points of view? Would

Table P-1
Composition of Focus Groups

	Focus Group 1	Focus Group 2	Focus Group 3
Type	Face to face	Online	Face to face
Total	6	12	5
Race/ ethnicity	2 African American 2 Puerto Rican 2 White	3 African American 1 Chinese American 3 Mexican American 5 White	5 South Asian

we keep our explicit promise to respect women's anonymity and our implicit promise to believe what they said?

We gained credibility with women leaders by approaching them through formal and informal professional networks. We had existing relationships with some of the women leaders, having served together on boards, commissions, or community projects. Others knew us by reputation at our own institutions or as leaders of national organizations.[11] Intermediaries or common acquaintances helped us approach women whose paths we had not crossed before. One result of our use of professional networks was that focus group participants often knew each other, whether directly or indirectly, before joining the group. Existing relationships between and among focus group participants contributed to a sense of comfort and community, expediting the engagement process.[12]

We invited women leaders to participate in one of three focus groups, with two of the groups meeting face-to-face and one of the groups meeting online. To create safe environments for discussing sensitive topics, we used principles from social group work and empowerment practice in composing the focus groups.[13] In racially and ethnically heterogeneous groups, we followed the "majority–minority" principle, inviting fewer white women per group than women leaders of color. We also followed the "Noah's ark" principle by inviting at least two women per focus group from the same racial or ethnic background. Our attempts to reach diverse women leaders were not always realized, however. Not all women who received invitations agreed to participate, and not all who accepted invitations actually took part. Women from First Nations did not accept invitations to the focus groups, and in retrospect, we may have needed an indigenous intermediary to help us locate and invite women leaders from First Nations.

We used this approach in composing a focus group for South Asian American women leaders. We were interested in the career paths of women leaders who were first-generation Americans, and a colleague who is herself a South Asian woman leader helped us locate and invite participants to a focus group for South

Asian women leaders in human services and the helping professions. All the women in this focus group had immigrated to the United States as adults or young adults following the Immigration Act of 1965. Relatively few South Asians of this generation are social workers in the United States, and of the five women leaders in the focus group, only two were employed in human services. The other three were scientists or engineers. All the South Asian women were active volunteers and community leaders, however. They had served as founders and directors of SNEHA (see chapter 6), a private, nonprofit organization that provides social, educational, and referral services to women of South Asian origin, exemplifying an alternative, culturally sensitive approach to human services.[14]

In planning the focus groups, we attempted to replicate the focus group process for the two groups meeting face-to-face and the group meeting online.[15] We sent written invitations and consent forms to the women leaders, explaining the process and purpose of the research and promising anonymity to participants. In the two face-to-face focus groups, participants signed and submitted the consent forms at the beginning of the focus group session. In the online group, participants entered the discussion by means of an online consent form. They indicated their agreement with the terms of the consent form (clicking on "agree") before gaining access to the discussion.

The face-to-face groups met for 90 minutes. One focus group met in conjunction with a national professional conference; the South Asian women leaders met on a college campus. The online group met by means of a password-protected message board over a two- to three-week period. Like face-to-face participants, online participants had the opportunity to introduce themselves before the formal discussion began (although we never figured out how to serve them refreshments). We posed the same set of semistructured questions, as listed in the appendix, to each group. For the online focus group, a new question was posted every two days. Participants could read and respond to one another's comments, and they could return to and continue with earlier parts of the discussion. Women in face-to-face groups were free to raise issues for discussion, and similarly, online participants could post their own questions or discussion topics.

More women accepted invitations to participate in the online group than the face-to-face groups, and as a result, the online group, with 12 members, was twice as large as the others. Several of the women in the online group experienced, but resolved, initial difficulties with the technology; technological problems prevented one woman from taking part. Once they entered the discussion, women in the online group, like those in the face-to-face groups, engaged in lively conversation, responding thoughtfully and eloquently to our questions and to the comments of other women.

As facilitators, we were present in the face-to-face focus groups, but we tried to intrude as little as possible beyond posing the questions. A graduate student moderated the online group, providing participants with technological support as needed. We audiotaped the face-to-face discussions and later transcribed the tapes. Transcripts of the online groups were saved and printed out. At the conclusion of the group sessions, we invited participants to write or e-mail us with any further thoughts or comments that they wanted to add. We sent written thank-you notes to all participants.

After conducting the three focus groups, we reviewed the transcripts to identify recurring language, patterns of language, and themes.[16] We organized the manuscript around those themes that recurred in the three focus groups or in the comments of most women from the same racial or ethnic backgrounds. The focus group discussions were rich in themes about how the women advanced into leadership positions and how they are leading human services organizations. Recurring themes in the women's approach to leadership suggested an approach that we call "leading from an inclusive perspective."

To engage our readers, we looked in the transcripts not only for recurring themes, but also for illustrative stories—short, discrete narratives with a beginning and ending as told in the women's own words. The difference between themes and stories is that themes are general, while stories are quite specific. Although we found many stories about the women's career development, there were few stories, or few that we could use, about the women's experiences as leaders. Specific examples of leadership often revealed the identities of women in highly visible positions. Having promised anonymity to focus group participants, we were reluctant to repeat stories that held identifying information about the women or their organizations.

Fortunately, as a university president, coauthor Karen Haynes had leadership stories to share. She was willing to speak on the record as a "situated actor" in our study of women leaders.[17] We decided to add Karen's stories to those of our focus groups, using Karen's diary and oral narrative interviews as primary sources.[18]

As explained by oral historian Gwendolyn Etter-Lewis, our responsibility in conducting focus groups was to listen well and "to cooperate in constructing a text that is fully representative" of the women's lives.[19] How well did we listen to the focus groups? How fairly did we present their experiences? With these questions in mind, we invited women of color from each of the focus groups to review a draft of the manuscript. The three readers, an African American, a Mexican American, and a South Asian woman leader, told us that the manuscript gave an accurate record of the context and content of their focus group discussions, presenting the women's stories "in authentic voice."

We wondered, however, about the stories that other women leaders have to tell.[20] How do the experiences of women in our focus groups compare with the experiences of other women leaders in human services, including their paths to leadership, their skills in resisting prejudice and discrimination, and their approaches to leading social change within and beyond their organizations? How does social work education prepare women for leadership careers?

According to Joan Acker and her colleagues, organizational researchers often accept a "hierarchy of oppressions."[21] They find it difficult to attend to issues of race, ethnicity, class, sex, and sexual orientation at the same time. In human services organizations, similarly, social workers sometimes fall into "competing

oppressions," finding it difficult to promote equity for all communities with equal care. The women in our focus groups learned
to transcend or expand their social identities to include many communities and groups. How does social work education teach this
capacity for becoming "citizens of the world"?

In its standards for culturally competent practice, NASW calls
on social workers to serve as cross-cultural leaders, "to share
information about diverse populations with the general public,
and to advocate for their clients' concerns at interpersonal and
institutional levels, locally, nationally, and internationally."[22]
How does social work education prepare cross-cultural leaders?
What experiences do students gain in creating inclusive, affirmative, equitable organizations; in opening educational and professional access to underrepresented groups; and in creating
environments where people work well, as a matter of course, in
multicultural teams?

According to Joyce Fletcher, organizational researchers sometimes attribute the success of women leaders to their personali-
ties rather than to their skills.[23] How does social work education
teach skills valued by the women in our focus groups, such as
skills in building professional resilience, in forming networks,
and in balancing multiple roles? How do we teach the capacity
for optimism, for meeting obstacles with perseverance and hope?
Women in our focus groups attributed professional knowledge,
skills, and values, including bicultural and multicultural understanding, to their families and their various communities. How
do schools of social work draw from students' families and communities, and how do we cultivate new communities as sources
of wisdom and support?[24] Above all, the women leaders referred
to the values that guided them in their personal and professional
lives. How does social work education affirm the values and
goals that first attract students to human services and then sustain them through their careers?

If we are to prepare women as leaders in human services,
then as educators, researchers, and leaders ourselves, we need to
talk and write about our visions for social work, however ideal-
istic they may seem, and to work day to day toward realizing

them. Like the women in our focus groups, we need to name our strengths: "I am a value added"; to claim our purpose: "We are a relentless force for change"; and to live by our examples. We are grateful to the women leaders for their examples. Although our work, like theirs, is a work in progress, we hope to have done them justice with this book.

Appendix

❧

Focus Group Questions

Women leaders in the focus groups responded to the following questions:

Expectations

- What were your goals and expectations when you began your career?
- What were the sources of your goals and expectations?

Relationships

- How have relationships helped you in your career?
- Have you found support from mentors or networks?

Loneliness

- Have you experienced loneliness in your profession?
- How have you dealt with being the only one or one of a few women (or women from your background) at various points in your career?

Mulitiple Roles

- How have you integrated personal and professional values and goals?
- How has biculturality or multiculturality helped or hindered your professional advancement?

Barriers

- What have been the barriers to your professional advancement?
- How have you overcome them?

Success

- Do you think of yourself as professionally successful?
- How do you define success?

Advice

- What advice do you have to prospective women leaders in human services?
- How have you helped or might you help prospective women leaders?

Notes

Notes to Preface

1. See, for example, Carlton-LaNey, 2001; Etter-Lewis, 1993; Hartman, 1999; Pantoja, 2002; Reid-Merritt, 1996.

2. See, for example, Blake-Beard, 1999; Catalyst, 1999a, 1999b; Federal Glass Ceiling Commission, 1995; Rosener, 1995; Ruderman & Ohlott, 2002; Swiss, 1996. Women of color are invisible in much organizational literature, according to Bell & Nkomo, 2001; Chow, 1994; Collins, 1997; Cox & Nkomo, 1990; Ferdman, 1999; Hurtado, 1999; Segura, 1994; Woo, 2000; Wu, 1997.

3. Healy, Havens, & Pine, 1995. See also Evans, 2000; Hollands, 2001.

4. Bell & Nkomo, 2001. See also Bell, Meyerson, Nkomo, & Scully, 2001; Catalyst, 1999b; Hurtado, 1999; Lambert & Hopkins, 1995.

5. Acker, 1999; Catalyst, 1999b; Daly, 1998; Ely, 1999; Hurtado, 1999; Marks, Hassim, January-Bardill, Khumalo, & Olekers, 2000; Rao, Rieky, & Kelleher, 1999; Thomas, 1996.

6. National Association of Social Workers, 1999, Preamble. See also the International Federation of Social Workers, 2002, proposed Statement of Ethics in Social Work: "The social work profession promotes

153

social change, problem solving in human relationships and the empowerment and liberation of people to enhance well-being."

7. Barker, 2003, p. 204.

8. International Federation of Social Workers, 2002.

9. Gibelman, 2003.

10. Austin, 1995; Gibelman, 2003; Ginsberg, 1995.

11. National Association of Social Workers, 2001, p. 29.

12. Haynes, 1989.

13. The backgrounds of focus group participants are summarized in
chapter 1, Table 1-1.

14. For a discussion of the focus group process, please see the postscript to this book. Questions asked of the focus groups are listed in the
appendix.

15. The professional positions of focus group participants are summarized in chapter 1, Table 1-2.

16. Social researchers interested in empowerment practice recom-
mend including research subjects as collaborators and active participants in defining the process and content of study. See, for example,
Altpeter, Schopler; Galinsky, & Pennell, 1999; Campfens, 1997; Finn,
1994; Friere, 1973; Gaventa, 1993; Gutiérrez, 1990; Gutiérrez & Lewis,
1999; Lee, 2001; Longres & Scanlon, 2001; Maguire, 1987. From a
postmodern perspective, researchers and research subjects collaborate
to reveal subjugated knowledge, as discussed in Brotman & Kraniou,
1999; Derrida, 1974; Foucault, 1980; Hartman, 1992; Reinharz, 1992;
Schriver, 1995; Scott, 1988.

17. Boyer, 1996, defined this kind of research and writing as "the
scholarship of integration" (p. 21). "Interdisciplinary, interpretive and
integrative," the scholarship of integration "fits one's own research or
the research of others into larger intellectual patterns" (p. 21), making
specialized knowledge accessible to people who are not specialists themselves. Wright, Euster, Gardella, Pollard, & Shulman, 2000, considered
the implications for social work education.

18. Erkut, 2001.

19. Hewlett, 2002, advised professional women not to sacrifice motherhood for careers, attracting widespread media attention. For other
examples of research on work, family, and gender, see Crosby, 1991;
Greenhaus & Parasuraman, 2000; Hochschild, 1989, 1997; Moen,
1992; Ortíz, 1996; Sprang, Secret, & Bradford, 1999; Young & Wright,
2001; Zedeck, 1992. Negative views of family have distinguished white

feminists and feminists of color, according to Holvino, 2001. See, for example, Higginbotham & Weber, 1992; Naples, 1997; Reid-Merritt, 1996; Romero, 1997.

20. Collins, 1990.

21. Anzaldúa, 1989; Bell, 1990; Bell & Nkomo, 1999; Blake-Beard, 1999; Bond, 1997; Castillo, 1994; Collins, 1997; Comas-Diaz & Greene, 1994; Daly, Jennings, Beckett, & Leashore, 1995; Lorde, 1984; Nkomo, 1996; Raman, 1999; Scott, 1991.

22. Heilbrun, 1988, p. 22. See also Etter-Lewis, 1993, p. xvi; Tannen, 1990; Vaz, 1997a.

‿ঌ৲‿ঌ৲‿ঌ৲

Notes to Chapter 1

1. Escúchenos. (2000, November 17). Conference of Connecticut Unido Para Niños Latinos, University of Connecticut School of Social Work, West Hartford, CT.

2. Joyner, 2001, p. 6.

3. Bordo, 1990, explains that researchers must struggle against racism and ethnocentrism while also accepting the impossibility of being fully inclusive in any one piece of research. "All ideas are condemned to be haunted by a voice from the margins . . . Our task is not to by stymied or halted by such voices but rather to be attentive to them" (p. 138).

4. As defined by Barker, 2003, p. 204, human services organizations plan, develop, manage, and provide services in the areas of social services, health, education, housing, income, justice, and public safety. In addition, human services organizations promote community and social development, economic development, and civil and human rights. Most U.S. human services organizations are in the public or nonprofit private sector, although states and local governments are increasingly contracting with private profit-making businesses to manage and provide human services.

5. Gibelman, 1999; Lewin, 2001; O'Neill, 2001.

6. Gibelman, 1999.

7. Gibelman, 1999, p. 409. See also Reskin, 1998, 1999.

8. Leighninger, 1987.

9. Americans United for Affirmative Action, 2000; Reskin, 1998, p. 17. Executive Order 11246, issued in 1965, applied to contracts worth more than $10,000.

10. English & Ross-Sheriff, 1998, p. 22.
11. Gardella, 1999.
12. Garza, 1993; Medina & Luna, 2000.
13. DiPalma & Topper, 2001.

$$\mathscr{L}\mathscr{L}\mathscr{L}$$

Notes to Chapter 2

1. Gutiérrez & Lewis, 1999, discuss the importance of religion and spirituality to women of color and their families. For a study of family and spirituality within religious traditions, see Van Hook, Hugen, & Aguilar, 2002.

2. Hanmer & Statham, 1989, p. 7. See also, for example, Billingsley, 1992; Collins, 2000b; Malson, Mudimbe-Boyi, O'Barr, & Wyer, 1988; Scott, 1991; Vaz, 1995. For a reminder of the changing structures of families and communities, see Gardella, 1999; Gross, 1999.

3. Lorde, 1981.

4. Hodges, 2001, p. 211. The National Association of Colored Women was founded in 1896 by Mary Church Terrell. See also Lorde, 1981. Bell & Nkomo, 2001, describe African American women's historical perspective on their communities: "Their communities sustain Black women in their work—not just the community that sustains them today, but the community of yesterday, their community of origin. . . . The intergenerational passing of the baton focuses their efforts on giving back to a collectivity" (p. 187).

5. Lewis, 1999, p. 164. See also hooks, 1994; Nagel, 1994.

6. Gutiérrez & Suarez, 1999. See also Medina & Luna, 2000; Ortíz, 1997; Torruellas, Benmayor, & Juarbe, 1996.

7. Gutiérrez & Suarez, 1999, p. 174. For discussions of intergenerational dynamics, see Blea, 1997; Candales, 2000; Gil & Vazquez, 1996; Mergal, 1993; Ramos, 1994.

8. Desai, D'Souza, & Shukla, 1999.

9. Prashad, 2000.

10. Desai et al., 1999; Flynn-Saulnier, 1996; Shah, 1997.

11. Van Den Bergh & Cooper, 1986. See also Flynn-Saulnier, 1996; Healy, Havens, & Pine, 1995; Hooyman & Cunningham, 1986; Weil, 1986.

12. Rank & Hutchison, 2000.

13. Mizrahi & Rosenthal, 2001.

14. Fletcher & Jacques, 1999. See also Fletcher, 1999a, 1999b; Merrill-Sands, Fletcher, Acosta, Andrews, & Harvey, 1999.

15. Hesselbein, 1999.

16. Wheatley, 1999, p. 39. For a study of participatory leadership, see Iannello, 1992.

ᘍᘍᘍ

Notes to Chapter 3

1. Jamieson, 1995, p. 141. For descriptions of solo status in academic settings, see Jennings, Martin, & Vroom, 1998; Medina & Luna, 2000; Nieves-Squires, 1991; Padilla & Chavez, 1995.

2. Biernat & Kobrynowicz, 1997. In this prejudiced worldview, successful individuals from minority groups are seen as overachievers. They have transcended their limited abilities by working exceptionally hard. For an excellent study of stereotyping, see Marks, Hassim, January-Bardill, Khumalo, & Olckers, 2000.

3. Shaw, 1996. See also Bailey, Wolfe, & Wolfe, 1996; Brown, Parker-Dominguez, & Sorey, 2000; Carlton-LaNey, 1999, 2001; Carlton-LaNey & Burwell, 1996; Collins, 1990; Etter-Lewis, 1993; Lambert & Hopkins, 1995; Lewis, 1999; Vaz, 1995.

4. Billingsley, 1992; Collins, 2000b; Hanmer & Statham, 1989; Malson, Mudimbe-Boyi, O'Barr, & Wyer, 1988; Reid-Merritt, 1996; Scott, 1991; Vaz, 1995.

5. Bell, Meyerson, Nkomo, & Scully, 2001; Bell & Nkomo, 2001.

6. Longres, 2000, p. 76, considers such groups "identificational communities" or "communities of interest" that are based on people's shared affection, allegiance, and sense of common identity and historical experience.

7. Federal Glass Ceiling Commission, 1995, p. 143. See also Catalyst, 1998, 1999a, 1999b.

8. Federal Glass Ceiling Commission, 1995, p. 3.

9. Federal Glass Ceiling Commission, 1995, p. 11. The commission was established pursuant to Title II of the Civil Rights Act of 1991.

10. Catalyst, 1999b.

11. Federal Glass Ceiling Commission, 1995, p. 6.

12. Catalyst, 1999b, p. 4; Federal Glass Ceiling Commission, 1995, pp. 58, 69, 86, 122; Woo, 2000, p. 47. Kivel & Wells, 1998, describe

the lavender ceiling as "invisibility in the underlying assumption that everyone is heterosexual; fear of intimidation and of loss of one's job; silencing through the inability to share in discussions about one's personal life; the creation and implementation of policies that do not represent or include nonheterosexual marriages or relationships; and fear for one's personal safety as a result of physical threats of violence." (pp. 109–110)

13. Federal Glass Ceiling Commission, 1995, pp. 8, 112. The commission noted, for example, that "acceptance of traditional stereotypes of women has influenced middle managers to move women to staff rather than to the line jobs" (p. 112) that lead to promotion.

14. Woo, 2000, p. 68. See also Federal Glass Ceiling Report, 1995.

15. Kolb, Fletcher, Meyerson, Merrill-Sands, & Ely, 1998; Rao, Rieky, & Kelleher, 1999.

16. In studies of occupational segregation related to sex, race, and ethnicity, Reskin found that employers use race and ethnicity to predict job performance, a practice exacerbated by the subjectivity and vague criteria of performance evaluations. See, for example, Reskin, 1998, p. 33; Reskin, 1999, p. 191.

17. Rao et al., 1999, p. 4.

18. Zweigenhaft & Domhoff, 1998, p. 52. Golf also affects women leaders in human services organizations. Deans of social work schools traditionally play golf at the annual meeting of the National Association of Deans and Directors.

19. Collins, 1990. See also Bell & Nkomo, 1999; Thomas, Phillips, & Brown, 1998.

20. Fletcher, 1999b. Marks, Hassim, January-Bardill, Khumalo, & Olekers, 2000, explain that "institutions both constitute and reproduce relations of power in society" (p. iii).

21. Gibelman, 1999; Lewin, 2001; O'Neill, 2001; Swiss, 1996.

22. Catalyst, 1999b, p. 21. See also Bell & Nkomo, 2001, p. 132; Blake-Beard, 1999, 2001a; Block & Carter, 1998.

23. Blake-Beard, 1999, 2001a; Crosby, 1999; Hurtado, 1989; Kelly & Post, 1995; Swiss, 1996; Thomas, 1989.

24. Catalyst, 1999b; Collins, Kamya, & Tourse, 1997; Loden, 1995.

25. Kelly & Post, 1995; Raggins, 1999; Swiss, 1996; Thomas, 1998.

26. Catalyst, 1999b, pp. 29–33.

27. Thomas, 1998. Other research on the significance of race and ethnicity in mentoring relationships includes that by Bell & Nkomo, 2001; Blake-Beard, 2001a; Block & Carter, 1998; Collins et al., 1997;

Murrell, Crosby, & Ely, 1999; Raggins, 1999; Thomas, 1989, 1998, 2001. For research on mentoring in academic settings, see Wilson, Valentine, & Pereira, 2002, who found race and ethnicity one among many factors contributing to successful mentoring.

28. Catalyst, 1998, 1999a; Catalyst, 1999b, pp. 75–99; Federal Glass Ceiling Commission, 1995, pp. 39–57; Wellington & Catalyst, 2001.

29. Researchers with the Center for Gender in Organizations call these individualistic approaches to change "fix-the-woman" and changes in formal organizational policies and practices "leveling the playing field," as in Kolb et al., 1998. See also Blake-Beard, 2001b; Rao et al., 1999. Chapter 6 further explores approaches to changing underlying prejudices and beliefs in the deep structure or organizational culture of human services organizations.

30. Kelly & Post, 1995; Swiss, 1996; Thomas, 1998; Van Den Bergh, 1998; Wilson et al., 2002.

31. Catalyst, 1999a; Van Den Bergh, 1998.

32. Kolb et al., 1998; Rao et al., 1999; Thomas, 1996.

ঌ৴ঌ৴ঌ৴

Notes to Chapter 4

1. Hewlett, 2002.

2. Greenhaus & Parasuraman, 2000; Hewlett, 2002; Hochschild, 1989, 1997; Moen, 1992; Sprang, Secret, & Bradford, 1999; Williams, 2000; Young & Wright, 2001; Zedeck, 1992. Negative views of family have distinguished white feminists from feminists of color, according to Holvino, 2001. Browne, 1999, has addressed work–family balance in working-class families.

3. Erkut, 2001.

4. Collins, 2000b. See also Castillo, 1994; Collins, 2000b; Crosby, 1991; Erkut, 2001.

5. Medina & Luna, 2000, p. 56.

6. García-Gorena, 2001; Glazer & Glazer, 2001; Naples, 1997.

7. For discussions of intergenerational dynamics, see Candales, 2000; Gil & Vazquez, 1996; Gutiérrez & Suarez, 1999; Min & Kim, 1999.

8. See, for example, Purkayastha, Raman, & Bhide, 1997. Women leaders developed culturally sensitive services for South Asian women in Connecticut (see chapter 6).

9. Federal Glass Ceiling Commission, 1995. See chapter 3 for a discussion of these prejudices.

10. Gibson & Ogbu, 1991. See also Carlton-LaNey & Burwell, 1996, who use a historical lens to examine intergroup relationships between African American and white women in human services.

11. Cox, 1996; Raman, 1999. See also Triandis, 1996, who describes the cultural–historical context of bicultural experience as including "cultural distance, differences in levels of adaptation on perceptual variables, emotional effects of the history of inter-group relations, patterns of acculturation of relevant cultures, and the tendency of members of each cultural group to make isomorphic attributions" (p. 225) or to accept generalized views of other groups.

12. Jennings, Martin, & Vroom, 1998.

13. Anzaldúa, 1987, 1989; Bell, 1990; Bell, Denton, & Nkomo, 1993; Bell & Nkomo, 2001; Daly, Jennings, Beckett, & Leashore, 1995; Denton, 1990; Gil & Vazquez, 1996; Medina & Luna, 2000; Min & Kim, 1999; Sam, 2000; Shah, 1997; Woo, 2000.

14. English & Ross-Sheriff, 1998; Lackland, 2000.

15. According to Longres, 2000, p. 76, identificational communities are based on people's shared affection, allegiance, and sense of common identity and historical experience.

16. Lackland, 2000; Min & Kim, 1999; Sam, 2000.

17. Bell & Nkomo, 2001, described cultural markers used by African American women in corporate management, such as wearing ethnic jewelry and displaying ethnic artwork in their offices.

18. Gutiérrez & Lewis, 1999. See also Fay, 1987; Friere, 1973; Gutiérrez, 1990; Lee, 2001; Pinderhughes, 1989; Solomon, 1976, 1987.

19. See, for example, Harragan, 1977; Hennig & Jardim, 1977; Molloy, 1977.

20. Evans, 2000.

21. Hollands, 2001.

22. Healy, Havens, & Pine, 1995, p. 133.

23. Fisher, Ury, & Patton, 1992; Kolb & Williams, 2000; Mindell, 1995; Tannen, 1996.

24. Kolb & Williams, 2000, p. 21.

25. Ely, 1999, p. 19.

26. Ely, 1999, p. 23.

27. Marks, Hassim, January-Bardill, Khumalo, & Olckers, 2000, p. 29. See also Bell & Nkomo, 2001; Ely & Thomas, 2000; Holvino, 2001; Hurtado, 1999; Kolb & Merrill-Sands, 1999.

28. Marks et al., 2000, p. 22. See also hooks, 2000. Acker, 1999, examines the invisibility of socioeconomic status or class in research on diversity in organizations, noting that in the United States, "class exploitation and inequity have far more legitimacy than gender and race-based exploitation and inequity, which are illegal and defined as discrimination in many countries" (p. 6).

29. Stoller & Gibson, 2000.

30. Healy, Havens, & Chin, 1990; Healy et al., 1995.

↬↬↬

Notes to Chapter 5

1. Wheatley, 1999, p. 144.

2. Chodorow, 1978. See also Jarrold & Lazzari, 2001; Jordan, 1997; Jordan, Kaplan, Miller, Stiver, & Surrey, 1991; Miller, 1991a; Miller & Stiver, 1997.

3. Miller, 1976. See also Collins, 2000a; Solomon, 1976, 1987.

4. Gilligan, 1982. See also Gilligan, Lyons, & Hanmer, 1990.

5. Belenky, Clinchy, Goldberger, & Tarule, 1986.

6. Noddings, 1984. See also Freedberg, 1993.

7. Jordan et al., 1991; Miller, 1991a; Miller & Stiver, 1997.

8. Miller & Stiver, 1997, p. 30. See also Fletcher & Jacques, 1999.

9. Fletcher & Jacques, 1999.

10. Helgeson, 1990. See also Loden, 1985; Rosener, 1995; Tannen, 1996; Weil, 1986.

11. Eagly & Johnson, 1990; Ely & Thomas, 2000; Healey, Havens, & Pine, 1995.

12. Miller, 1991b, p. 205.

13. Acker, 1999; Bell & Nkomo, 2001; Ely, 1999; Ely & Thomas, 2000; Holvino, 2001; Hurtado, 1999; Kolb & Merrill-Sands, 1999; Marks, Hassim, January-Bardill, Khumalo, & Olckers, 2000.

14. Brown, Parker-Dominguez, & Sorey, 2000, p. 56. See also Bond, 1997; Candales, 2000; Medina & Luna, 2000.

15. Higginbotham & Weber, 1999, suggested that just as white women managers generally are less aware of racial discrimination than African American women managers, women of color from one racial or ethnic group may not fully appreciate the particular forms of prejudice and discrimination experienced by women of color from different racial or ethnic groups.

16. Bulbeck, 1998; Purkayastha, Raman, & Bhide, 1997; Shah, 1997.

17. Tobitt, n.d. This song, suitably sung as a round, has the lyric, "Make new friends and keep the old; one is silver and the other, gold." Oral histories with other women leaders in social work document their skill in building lifelong support networks, as in Gardella, 1997, 1999.

18. Brown et al., 2000. These findings were constant for married, partnered, and single women.

19. Heilbrun, 1988.

20. Organizational researchers may be more likely than the women in our focus groups to distinguish between personal and professional relationships. As a result, they may miss the significance of women's friends as sources of professional support.

21. For example, according to Catalyst, 1999b, p. 21, "CEOs report having an influential mentor as the most significant factor in their own career advancement."

22. As discussed in chapter 3, researchers have found that mentors and mentees prefer mentoring partners of the same sex and race. See, for example, Catalyst, 1999b; Kelly & Post, 1995; Thomas, 1998. The racial and ethnic dimensions of mentoring relationships are considered in Bell & Nkomo, 2001; Blake-Beard, 2001a; Block & Carter, 1998; Catalyst, 1999b; Collins, Kamya, & Tourse, 1997; Loden, 1995; Murrell, Crosby, & Ely, 1999; Thomas, 1989, 1998, 2001; Wilson, Valentine, & Pereira, 2002.

23. Chapter 3 examines women's difficulties in finding mentors. See also Catalyst, 1999b; Federal Glass Ceiling Commission, 1995.

24. DiPalma & Topper, 2000.

25. Wenger & Snyder, 2000, p. 139.

26. Catalyst, 1999a; Swiss, 1996; Van Den Bergh, 1998.

27. Catalyst, 1998, 1999a.

28. Swiss, 1996. As an example of collective action, Swiss described a women's network that provides training seminars on negotiation for women managers in philanthropic organizations. The group, Women in Development of Greater Boston, 1992, publishes a negotiating manual with regional statistics on salaries and compensation packages. This insiders' information allows women managers to improve their bargaining positions and reduce inequities in the compensation of women and men.

꒦꒦꒦

Notes to Chapter 6

1. Myerson & Scully, 1999, p. 1. See also Bell, Meyerson, Nkomo, & Scully, 2001.

2. Glater, 2001.

3. The women leaders discussed their experiences of working in solo status in chapter 3. See also Jamieson, 1995. For a precautionary view, see Bell & Nkomo, 2001, p. 12, who suggest that hostility and stereotyping against African Americans in an organization may increase as African American professionals make numerical gains.

4. Havens & Healy, 1991. Healy, Havens, & Pine, 1995, pp. 136–137, discuss the symbolic importance of numbers, finding, for example, that as women assume senior leadership positions in an organization, middle managers are more likely to hire and promote other women into management roles.

5. Ely & Thomas, 2000, pp. 3–4.

6. Ely, 1999. For examples of playing the corporate game, see also Evans, 2000.

7. Marks, Hassim, January-Bardill, Khumalo, & Olekers, 2000, p. 20.

8. Zweigenhaft & Domhoff, 1998, p. 192.

9. Rao, Rieky, & Kelleher, 1999, p. 6.

10. Federal Glass Ceiling Commission, 1995; Marks et. al., 2000; Rao et al., 1999.

11. Thomas, 1996.

12. Thomas, 1996. According to Thomas, Phillips, & Brown, 1998, p. 76, organizations, like individuals, have ethnocentric worldviews. In corporate ethnocentrism, corporate cultures that favor historically dominant cultural groups fail to recognize barriers to other groups.

13. Chivers, 2001; Haney & Hurtado, 1994.

14. Catalyst, 1999b; Federal Glass Ceiling Commission, 1995; Kelly & Post, 1995; Reskin, 1998, 1999; Thomas, 1998; Woo, 2000.

15. Fletcher, 1999b. Universities assign more service activities to faculty of color than to white faculty, according to Garza, 1993; Medina & Luna, 2000; and the National Education Association, 1991. Tierney & Bensimon, 1996, describe these service expectations as "cultural taxation" (p. 115).

16. Fletcher, 1999b, p. 135.

17. Lewin, 2001.

18. Ely & Thomas, 2000.

19. SNEHA is a Hindi word that means "loving relationship," as explained by Purkayastha, Raman, & Bhide, 1997. Social services designed for ethnic communities are examined in Chow, 1999; Iglehart & Becerra, 2000. For discussions of cultural competence from global feminist perspectives, see Bulbeck, 1998; Shah, 1997.

20. SNEHA, Inc., n.d. Reprinted with permission.

21. Germain & Gitterman, 1996; Gutiérrez & Lewis, 1999; Lee, 2001.

22. Kolb, Fletcher, Meyerson, Merrill-Sands, & Ely, 1998; Rao et al., 1999.

23. Kolb et al., 1998; Rao et al., 1999.

24. Rao et al., 1999, p. 2.

25. Rao et al., 1999, p. 4.

26. Acker, 1999, p. 12.

27. Merrill-Sands, Fletcher, Acosta, Starks, Andrews, & Harvey, 1999, pp. 36–37. See also Ely, 1996.

28. Altpeter, Schopler, Galinsky, & Pennell, 1999; Campfens, 1997; DePoy, Hartman, & Haslett, 1999; Finn, 1994; Herr, 1995; Lewin, 1948; Longres & Scanlon, 2001; Reese, Ahern, Nair, O'Faire, & Warren, 1999; Whyte, 1991.

29. Catalyst, 1999a. See chapter 5 for a discussion of women's networks and ethnic affinity groups.

30. Meyerson & Fletcher, 2000. Meyerson and Fletcher attribute the "small wins" approach to Weick, 1984.

31. Campfens, 1997; Lee, 2001.

32. Hopkins, 1999.

33. A study on the status of women faculty in science at MIT, 1999, March.

34. Cox & Wilson, 2001.

35. According to Jacobson, 2001, of 1,637 tenured or tenure-track chemistry faculty in the top 50 U.S. chemistry departments in 2001, only seven were women of color.

ودودودو

Notes to Chapter 7

1. Rosener, 1995. See also Helgeson, 1990; Loden, 1985; Weil, 1986.

2. University of Houston–Victoria, 2001.

3. Bowlin, 2001a.

4. Bowlin, 2001b.

ぷぷぷ

Notes to Postscript

1. Miller, 1991b, p. 205.

2. Woo, 2000. According to Catalyst, 1999b, women corporate managers of color, particularly women of color from specific racial and ethnic groups, have been invisible in organizational research because they have advanced into management in small numbers.

3. Various journals have lamented the gap between social work research and practice. They have called for accessible research and writing that presents the viewpoints of practitioners and clients. See, for example, Feeney, 2000; Figueira-McDonough, Netting, & Nicols-Casebolt, 2001; Hartman, 1992; Schriver, 1995; Weick, 2000; Witkin, 2000. Weick, 2000, offers a useful definition of qualitative research when she recommends learning about social work practice "not from the framework of a theory constructed from the outside, but from the meaning developed from the inside" (p. 400).

4. National Association of Social Workers, 2001.

5. Bell, Meyerson, Nkomo, & Scully, 2001; Bell & Nkomo, 2001; Higginbotham & Weber, 1999; Hurtado, 1989. For a historical perspective, see Carlton-LaNey, 2000; Carlton-LaNey & Burwell, 1996; Lorde, 1981; Poster, 1995; Shaw, 1996.

6. See, for example, Beckett & Dungee-Anderson, 1998; Browne, 1999; Chow, 1994; Cox, 1996; Fabelo-Alcover & Sowers, 1998; Min & Kim, 1999; Prashad, 2000.

7. Cultural competence is part of social workers' ethical responsibilities to clients, as defined by the *NASW Code of Ethics*, 1999, Section 1.05. *NASW Standards for Cultural Competence in Social Work Practice*, 2001, includes standards related to ethics and values, self-awareness, cross-cultural knowledge and skills, service delivery, empowerment and advocacy, workforce diversity, professional education, language diversity, and cross-cultural leadership. In its *Educational Policy and Accreditation Standards*, the Council on Social Work Education, 2001, defines the purposes of the social work profession to include developing and applying practice "in the context of diverse cultures" (p. 5).

8. Appleby, 2001b, p. 20; Cox & Gallois, 1996, p. 12.

9. Dunn, 1998, pp. 80–81, calls this approach "integrative pluralism." See also Pennell and Ristock, 1999, p. 462, who call for "groundless solidarity," or removing both "oppressive classifications and universalizing theories" as impediments to social action. Anzaldúa

considers the possibility of transforming differences in Anzaldúa & Keating, 2002.

10. All researchers are subjective in the postmodern view, but power and privilege complicate matters for researchers from majority groups. Feminist standpoint theorists have considered these ideas, as discussed in Swigonski, 1994. Many researchers have explored the interrelationships of race, gender, class, and power in constructing knowledge and conducting research on organizations. See, for example, Collins, 1990, 1999; Cox, 1996; Ely, 1996; Gutiérrez, 1992; Gutiérrez, GlenMaye, & DeLois, 1995; Gutiérrez & Lewis, 1999; Morrison, 1992. Implications for focus group research are considered in Callaghan, 1998; Dreaschslin, 1998. Feminist theorists have considered the subjectivity of researchers and the power of dominant groups to control discourse, as in Davis, 1981; Davis, 1994; Denzin, 1989; Elam, 1994; Faderman, 1999; Fine, 1992; Heilbrun, 1988; hooks, 1984, 1989, 1994; Lather, 1991. For dominant groups' relative ignorance of minority groups, see Carter, 1998; Miller, 1976. Implications for white researchers are considered in Frankenberg, 1993; McIntosh, 1995; Rothenberg, 2000, 2001. As white researchers, we were at a disadvantage in understanding racism, but in a favorable position to protest against it. As Rothenberg, 2001, explains: "One very effective way of getting a hearing for any form of injustice is to ask each other's questions. . . . People are often puzzled and intrigued to hear a critique of white privilege coming from one who benefits from it" (p. 179).

11. We risked the possibility that participants' prior relationships would interfere with the group process or inhibit discussion; however, Wayne, 2002, recommends using snowball samples in focus group research with communities. For methodological issues in focus group composition, see Kidd & Parshall, 2000; Krueger & King, 1998; Morgan, 1998; Smith, 1995.

12. National professional networks helped us locate women leaders who came from various racial and ethnic backgrounds and from various geographic regions in the United States. At the same time, our use of networks limited the professional diversity in our focus groups because our networks consisted largely of women and men who currently were associated with higher education or social work education. All women in the focus groups had served as leaders of human services organizations at some point during their careers. The women leaders' backgrounds are summarized in chapter 1, Tables 1-1 and 1-2.

13. Lee, 2001, p. 289. Issues of engagement with racially and ethnically heterogeneous groups are explored in Bilides, 1990; Chau, 1990; Davis, 1985; Davis & Proctor, 1989; Dreachslin, 1998; Gitterman & Shulman, 1994; Gutiérrez & Lewis, 1999; Hopps & Pinderhughes, 1999.

14. For a discussion of SNEHA, see Purkayastha, Raman, & Bhide, 1997.

15. Much of the literature on online groups in social work concerns groups used in social work practice, as in Abell & Galinsky, 2002. Less attention has been given to the use of online groups for research. Appleby, 2001a, located and interviewed research subjects on the Internet in his international study of gay working-class men. Estes, 1999, gave an overview of Internet tools for social work research, while Lynch, Vernon, and Folaron, 2001, considered practical and ethical issues in conducting research on the Internet, such as evaluating Internet-based resources for validity and rigor and protecting the confidentiality and privacy of sources.

16. Coding or identifying themes in focus group research is explored in Catterall & Maclaran, 1997. See also Carey & Smith, 1994; Davies, 1999; Henderson, 1995; Jaeger, Schule, & Kasemir, 1999; Kidd & Parshall, 2000.

17. Hertz, 1997, p. 15, would consider this a qualitative research approach called "reflexive ethnography." Reflexive ethnographers study their experience as they are living it. The value of reflexivity in social research is further examined in Brotman & Kraniou, 1999; Creswell, 1998; Eakin, Robertson, Poland, Coburn, & Edwards, 1996; Gaventa, 1993; Jaeger et al., 1999.

18. For a discussion of qualitative research with personal documents, see Holbrook, 1995. The methodology of oral narrative research is examined in Etter-Lewis, 1993; Gardella, 1999; Martin, 1995; Vansina, 1985; Vaz, 1997a.

19. Etter-Lewis, 1993, p. xiv. We applied principles of oral narrative research to the focus groups. Although the women were telling their life stories in a group rather than in an individual interview, we wanted to present their stories authentically in their own words and voices. For the significance of using narrators' own language in qualitative research, see Etter-Lewis, 1993; Martin, 1995; Vansina, 1985; Vaz, 1997a.

20. Speaking as individuals, the women in our focus groups told small local stories. Small stories slow the rush to generalization, calling

attention to individual and intragroup differences and sometimes calling into question our assumptions about groups and about ourselves. As Pennell and Ristock, 1999, explain, "postmodern perspectives generate different stories, stories that prevent researchers and activists from assuming a posture of either absolute certainty of truth or incapacitating uncertainty of courses of action" (p. 461). For the value of small stories in studying diversity, see also Aptheker, 1989; Calás & Smircich, 1999; Lather, 1991.

 21. Acker, 1999; Ely, 1999; Hurtado, 1999; Marks et al., 2000.

 22. National Association of Social Workers, 2001, p. 29.

 23. Fletcher, 1999b.

 24. Parks, 2000.

Bibliography

Abell, M. L., & Galinsky, M. J. (2002). Introducing students to computer-based group work practice. *Journal of Social Work Education, 38*, 39–54.

Acker, J. (1999). *Revisiting class: Lessons from theorizing race and gender in organizations* (CGO Working Paper No. 5). Boston: Simmons Graduate School of Management, Center for Gender in Organizations.

Aguilar, M. A. (1996). Promoting the educational achievement of Mexican American young women. *Social Work in Education, 18*(3), 145–157.

Allen, M. L., Brown, P., & Finlay, B. (1992). *Helping children by strengthening families.* Washington, DC: Children's Defense Fund.

Altpeter, M., Schopler, J. H., Galinsky, M. J., & Pennell, J. (1999). Participatory research as social work practice: When is it viable? *Journal of Progressive Human Services, 10*(2), 31–53.

Americans United for Affirmative Action. (2000). Available online at www.auaa.org/timeline.

Anzaldúa, G. E. (1987). *Borderlands/La frontera: The new mestiza.* San Francisco: Spinsters/Aunt Lute Book Co.

Anzaldúa, G. E. (Ed.). (1989). *Making face, making soul/Haciendo caras: Creative and critical perspectives by feminists of color.* San Francisco: Aunt Lute Books.

Anzaldúa, G. E., & Keating, A. (Eds.). (2002). *This bridge we call home: Radical visions for transformation*. New York: Routledge.

Appleby, G. A. (2001a). Interviewing working-class gay men over the Internet. *Journal of Gay and Lesbian Social Services, 12*(3/4), 133–152.

Appleby, G. A. (2001b). Methodology: Framework for practice with working-class gay and bisexual men. *Journal of Gay and Lesbian Social Services, 12*(3/4), 5–46.

Appleby, G. A., & Anastas, J. W. (1998). *Not just a passing phase: Social work with gay, lesbian, and bisexual people*. New York: Columbia University Press.

Aptheker, B. (1989). *Tapestries of life: Women's work, women's consciousness, and the meaning of daily experience*. Amherst: University of Massachusetts Press.

Austin, D. M. (1995). Management overview. In R. L. Edwards (Ed.-in-Chief), *Encyclopedia of social work* (19th ed., Vol. 2, pp. 1642–1658). Washington, DC: NASW Press.

Bailey, D., Wolfe, D., & Wolfe, C. R. (1996). The contextual impact of social support across race and gender: Implications for African-American women in the workplace. *Journal of Black Studies, 26*(3), 297–303.

Barker, R. L. (2003). *The social work dictionary* (5th ed.). Washington, DC: NASW Press.

Beckett, J. O., & Dungee-Anderson, D. (1998). Multicultural communication in human services organizations. In A. Daly (Ed.), *Workplace diversity: Issues and perspectives* (pp. 191–215). Washington, DC: NASW Press.

Belenky, M. F., Clinchy, B. M., Goldberger, N. R., & Tarule, J. M. (1986). *Women's ways of knowing: The development of self, voice and mind*. New York: Basic Books.

Bell, E. L. (1990). The bicultural life experiences of career-oriented black women. The career and life experiences of black professionals [Special issue]. *Journal of Organizational Behavior, 11*, 459–464.

Bell, E. L., Denton, T. C., & Nkomo, S. (1993). Women of color in management: Toward an inclusive analysis. In E. A. Fagenson (Ed.), *Women in management: Trends, issues, and challenges in managerial diversity* (pp. 105–130). Newbury Park, CA: Sage Publications.

Bell, E. L., Meyerson, D., Nkomo, S., & Scully, M. (2001). *Tempered radicalism revisited: Black and white women making sense of black women's enactments and white women's silences* (CGO Working Paper No. 13). Boston: Simmons Graduate School of Management, Center for Gender in Organizations.

Bell, E. L., & Nkomo, S. M. (1999). Postcards from the Borderlands: Building a career from the outside/within. *Journal of Career Development, 26*(1), 69–84.

Bell, E. L., & Nkomo, S. M. (2001). *Our separate ways: Black and white women and the struggle for professional identity.* Boston: Harvard Business School Press.

Biernat, M., & Kobrynowicz, D. (1997). Gender- and race-based standards of competence: Lower minimum standards but higher ability standards for devalued groups. *Journal of Personal and Social Psychology, 73,* 544–557.

Bilides, D. G. (1990). Race, color, ethnicity and class: Issues of biculturalism in school-based adolescent counseling groups. *Social Work with Groups, 13*(4), 43–58.

Billingsley, A. (1992). *Climbing Jacob's ladder: The enduring legacy of African American families.* New York: Simon & Schuster.

Billups, J. O. (Ed.). (2002). *Faithful angels: Portraits of international social work notables.* Washington, DC: NASW Press.

Blake-Beard, S. D. (1999). The costs of living as an outsider within: An analysis of the mentoring relationships and career success of black and white women in the corporate sector. *Journal of Career Development, 26*(1), 21–36.

Blake-Beard, S. D. (2001a). *Mentoring relationships through the lens of race and gender* (CGO Insights No. 10). Boston: Simmons Graduate School of Management, Center for Gender in Organizations.

Blake-Beard, S. D. (2001b). Taking a hard look at formal mentoring programs: A consideration of potential challenges facing women. *Journal of Management Development, 20*(4), 331–345.

Blea, I. I. (1997). Chicana feminist movement. In I. I. Blea (Ed.), *U.S. Chicanas & Latinas within a global context.* Westport, CT: Praeger.

Block, C. J., & Carter, R. T. (1998). Mentoring and diversity in organizations: Importance of race and gender in work relationships. In A. Daly (Ed.), *Workplace diversity: Issues and perspectives* (pp. 281–292). Washington, DC: NASW Press.

Bond, M. A. (1997). The multitextured lives of women of color. *American Journal of Community Psychology 25*(5), 737–738.

Bordo, S. (1990). Feminism, postmodernism, and gender-skepticism. In L. G. Nicholson (Ed.), *Feminism/postmodernism* (pp. 133–156). New York: Routledge.

Bowlin, S. (2001a, May 18). Making college accessible is program's aim. *Victoria Advocate,* pp. 6A, 7A.

Bowlin, S. (2001b, May 18). Rangers to the rescue: Mentoring program is a refuge for students needing a guiding hand. *Victoria Advocate*, p. 3A.

Boyer, E. L. (1996). *Scholarship reconsidered: Priorities of the professoriate*. Princeton, NJ: The Carnegie Foundation for the Advancement of Teaching.

Bracy, W. D., & Cunningham, M. (1995). Factors contributing to the retention of minority students: Implications for incorporating diversity. *Journal of Baccalaureate Social Work, 1*(1), 85–96.

Brotman, S., & Kraniou, S. (1999). Ethnic and lesbian: Understanding identity through the life-history approach. *Affilia, 14,* 417–438.

Brown, K.A.E., Parker-Dominguez, T. P., & Sorey, M. (2000). Life stress, social support, and well-being among college-educated African American women. *Journal of Ethnic and Cultural Diversity in Social Work, 9*(1/2), 55–73.

Browne, I. (Ed.). (1999). *Latinas and African American women at work: Race, gender, and economic inequality*. New York: Russell Sage Foundation.

Bulbeck, C. (1998). *Re-orienting Western feminisms: Women's diversity in a postcolonial world*. Cambridge, England: Cambridge University Press.

Calás, M. B., & Smircich, L. (1999). Past postmodernism? Reflections and tentative directions. *Academy of Management Review, 24,* 649–671.

Callaghan, G. (1998). The interaction of gender, class and place in women's experience: A discussion based in focus group research. *Sociological Research Online, 3*(3). Retrieved from www.socresonline.org.uk/socresonline/3/3/8.html on March 30, 2002.

Campfens, H. (1997). International review of community development: Theory and practice. In H. Campfens (Ed.), *Community development around the world: Practice, theory, research, training* (pp. 11–40). Toronto: University of Toronto Press.

Candales, B. A. (2000). *Nuestras historias (Our stories): Transformative learning among female Puerto Rican community college graduates*. Unpublished doctoral dissertation, University of Connecticut, Storrs.

Carey, M. A., & Smith, M. W. (1994). Capturing the group effect in focus groups: A special concern in analysis. *Qualitative Health Research, 4,* 123–127.

Carlton-LaNey, I. (1999). African American social work pioneers' response to need. *Social Work, 44*(4), 311–322.

Carlton-LaNey, I. (2000). Women and interracial cooperation in establishing the Good Samaritan Hospital. *Affilia, 15*, 65–81.

Carlton-LaNey, I. (Ed.). (2001). *African American leadership: An empowerment tradition in social welfare history*. Washington, DC: NASW Press.

Carlton-LaNey, I., & Burwell, N. Y. (1996). *African American community practice models: Historical and contemporary responses*. New York: Haworth Press.

Carter, R. T. (1998). *The influence of race and racial identity in psychotherapy: Toward a racially inclusive model*. New York: Wiley-InterScience.

Castillo, A. (1994). *Massacre of the dreamers*. New York: Plume.

Catalyst. (1998). *Advancing women in business—The Catalyst guide: Best practices from the corporate leaders*. San Franciso: Jossey-Bass.

Catalyst. (1999a). *Creating women's networks: A how-to guide for women and companies*. San Francisco: Jossey-Bass.

Catalyst. (1999b). *Women of color in corporate management: Opportunities and barriers*. New York: Author.

Catterall, M., & Maclaran, P. (1997). Focus group data and qualitative analysis programs: Coding the moving picture as well as the snapshots. *Sociological Research Online, 2*(1). Retrieved from www.socresonline.org.uk/socresonline/2/1/6.html on March 30, 2002.

Chau, K. (Ed.). (1990). *Ethnicity and biculturalism: Emerging perspectives of social group work*. New York: Haworth Press.

Chivers, C. J. (2001, April 12). For black officers, diversity has its limits. *New York Times*. Retrieved from www.nytimes.com on April 14, 2001.

Chodorow, N. (1978). *The reproduction of mothering: Psychoanalysis and the sociology of gender*. Berkeley: University of California Press.

Chow, E. N. (1994). Asian American women at work. In M. B. Zinn & B. T. Dill (Eds.), *Women of color in U.S. society*. Philadelphia: Temple University Press.

Chow, J. (1999). Multi-service centers in Chinese American immigrant communities: Practice principles and challenges. *Social Work, 44*, 70–81.

Collins, P. H. (1990). Learning from the outsider within: The sociological significance of black feminist thought. *Social Problems, 33*(6), 14–32.

Collins, P. H. (1999). Moving beyond gender: Intersectionality and scientific knowledge. In M. M. Feree, J. Lorger, & B. B. Hess

(Eds.), *Revisioning gender* (pp. 261–284). Thousand Oaks, CA: Sage Publications.

Collins, P. H. (2000a). *Black feminist thought: Knowledge, consciousness, and the politics of empowerment* (2nd ed.). New York: Routledge.

Collins, P. H. (2000b). It's all in the family: Intersection of gender, race, and nation. In U. Narayan & S. Harding (Eds.), *Decentering the center* (pp. 156–176). Bloomington: Indiana University Press.

Collins, P. M., Kamya, H. A., & Tourse, R. W. (1997). Questions of racial diversity and mentorship: An empirical exploration. *Social Work, 42*(2), 145–151.

Collins, S. (1997). Black mobility in white corporations: Up the ladder but out on a limb. *Social Problems, 44*(1), 59.

Comas-Diaz, L., & Greene, B. (1994). *Women of color: Integrating ethnic and gender identities in psychotherapy*. New York: Guilford Press.

Council on Social Work Education. (2001). *Educational policy and accreditation standards*. Alexandria, VA: Author.

Cox, A. M., & Wilson, R. (2001, February 9). Leaders of 9 universities pledge to improve conditions for female scientists. *Chronicle of Higher Education, 17*(22), p. A12.

Cox, S., & Gallois, C. (1996). Gay and lesbian identity development: A social identity perspective. *Journal of Homosexuality, 30*(4), 1–30.

Cox, T., Jr. (1994). *Cultural diversity in organizations: Theory, research and practice*. San Francisco: Berrett-Koehler.

Cox, T., Jr. (1996). The complexity of diversity: Challenges and directions for future research. In S. E. Jackson & M. N. Ruderman (Eds.), *Diversity in work teams: Research paradigms for a changing workplace* (pp. 235–246). Washington, DC: American Psychological Association.

Cox, T., Jr. (2001). *Creating the multicultural organization: A strategy for capturing the power of diversity*. San Francisco: Jossey-Bass.

Cox, T., Jr., & Nkomo, S. N. (1990). Invisible men and women: A status report on race as a variable in organizational behavioral research. *Journal of Organizational Behavior, 11*, 419–431.

Creswell, J. (1998). *Qualitative inquiry and research design: Choosing among five traditions*. Thousand Oaks, CA: Sage Publications.

Crosby, F. J. (1991). *Juggling: The unexpected advantages of balancing career and home for women and their families*. New York: Oxford University Press.

Crosby, F. J. (1999). The developmental literature on developmental relationships. In A. J. Murrell, F. J. Crosby, & R. J. Ely (Eds.), *Mentoring dilemmas: Developmental relationships within multicultural organizations.* Hillsdale, NJ: Lawrence Erlbaum.

Daly, A. (Ed.). (1998). *Workplace diversity: Issues and perspectives.* Washington, DC: NASW Press.

Daly, A., Jennings, J., Beckett, J., & Leashore, B. (1995). Effective coping strategies of African Americans. *Social Work, 40,* 240–248.

Davies, A. R. (1999). Where do we go from here? Environmental focus groups and planning policy formation. *Local Environment, 4*(3), 295–317.

Davis, A. (1981). *Women, race, and class.* New York: Random House.

Davis, L. E. (1984). *Ethnicity in social group work practice.* New York: Random House.

Davis, L. E. (1985). Group work practice with ethnic minorities of color. In M. Sundel, P. Glasser, R. Sarri, & R. Vinter (Eds.), *Individual change through small groups* (pp. 324–345). New York: Free Press.

Davis, L. E., & Proctor, E. K. (1989). *Race, gender, and class: Guidelines for working with individuals, families and groups.* Englewood Cliffs, NJ: Prentice Hall.

Davis, L. V. (Ed.). (1994). *Building on women's strengths: A social work agenda for the twenty-first century.* New York: Haworth Press.

Denton, T. C. (1990). Bonding and supportive relationships among black professional women: Rituals of restoration. The career and life experiences of black professionals [Special issue]. *Journal of Organizational Behavior, 11,* 447–457.

Denzin, N. K. (1989). *Interpretive biography.* Newbury Park, CA: Sage Publications.

DePoy, E., Hartman, A., & Haslett, D. (1999). Critical action research: A model of social work knowing. *Social Work, 44,* 560–570.

Derrida, J. (1974). *Of grammatology* (G. C. Spivak, Trans.). Baltimore: Johns Hopkins University Press.

Desai, D., D'Souza, N., & Shukla, S. (Eds.). (1999). *Indelible imprints: Daughters write on fathers.* Calcutta, India: Bhatkal Books International.

Devore, W., & Schlesinger, E. (1996). *Ethnic sensitive social work practice* (4th ed.). Boston: Allyn & Bacon.

DiPalma, S. L., & Topper, G. C. (2001). Social work academia: Is the glass ceiling beginning to crack? *Affilia, 16,* 31–45.

Dreachslin, J. L. (1998). Conducting effective focus groups in the context of diversity: Theoretical underpinnings and practical implications. *Qualitative Health Research, 8,* 813–901.

Duerst-Lahti, G., & Kelly, R. M. (Eds.). (1995). *Gender, power, leadership, and governance.* Ann Arbor: University of Michigan Press.

Dunn, E. F. (1998). Historical review of U.S. policy on diversity. In A. Daly (Ed.), *Workplace diversity: Issues and perspectives* (pp. 70–87). Washington, DC: NASW Press.

Eagly, A. H., & Johnson, B. T. (1990). Gender and leadership style: A meta-analysis. *Psychological Bulletin, 108,* 233–256.

Eakin, J., Robertson, A., Poland, B., Coburn, D., & Edwards, R. (1996). A critical social science perspective on health promotion research. *Health Promotion International, 11,* 157–165.

Elam, D. (1994). *Feminism and deconstruction.* New York: Routledge.

Ely, R. J. (1996). The role of dominant identity and experience in organizational work on diversity. In S. E. Jackson & M. N. Ruderman (Eds.), *Diversity in work teams: Research paradigms for a changing workplace* (pp. 161–186). Washington, DC: American Psychological Association.

Ely, R. J. (1999). *Feminist critiques of research on gender in organizations* (CGO Working Paper No. 6). Boston: Simmons Graduate School of Management, Center for Gender in Organizations.

Ely, R. J., & Thomas, D. A. (2000). *Cultural diversity at work: The moderating effects of work group perspectives on diversity* (CGO Working Paper No. 10). Boston: Simmons Graduate School of Management, Center for Gender in Organizations.

English, R. A., & Ross-Sheriff, F. (1998). Diversity and challenges of new immigrants in the changing American workforce. In A. Daly (Ed.), *Workplace diversity: Issues and perspectives* (pp. 21–35). Washington, DC: NASW Press.

Erkut, S. (2001). *Inside women's power: Learning from leaders.* Wellesley, MA: Wellesley College Center for Research on Women.

Estes, R. (1993). Toward sustainable development: From theory to praxis. *Social Development Issues, 15*(3), 1–19.

Estes, R. (1999). Informational tools for social workers: Research in the global age. In C. S. Ramanathan & R. J. Link (Eds.), *All our futures: Principles and resources for social work practice in a global era* (pp. 121–137). Pacific Grove, CA: Brooks/Cole.

Etter-Lewis, G. (1993). *My soul is my own: Oral narratives of African American women in the professions.* New York: Routledge.

Evans, G. (2000). *Play like a man, win like a woman*. New York: Broadway Books.

Fabelo-Alcover, H. E., & Sowers, K. M. (1998). Latino diversity in communication in the workplace. In A. Daly (Ed.), *Workplace diversity: Issues and perspectives* (pp. 215–228). Washington, DC: NASW Press.

Faderman, L. (1999). *To believe in women: What lesbians have done for America—A history*. Boston: Houghton Mifflin.

Fay, B. (1987). *Critical social science: Liberation and its limits*. Ithaca, NY: Cornell University Press.

Federal Glass Ceiling Commission. (1995). *Good for business: Making full use of the nation's human capital. The environmental scan*. Washington, DC: Author.

Feeney, S. (2000). Introduction: Special issue on symposium. Authority, legitimacy, voice, and the scholar-practice question. *Nonprofit and Voluntary Sector Quarterly, 29*(1), 5–10.

Ferdman, B. M. (1999). The color and culture of gender in organizations. In G. N. Powell (Ed.), *Handbook of gender and work*. Thousand Oaks, CA: Sage Publications.

Figueira-McDonough, J., Netting, F. E., & Nicols-Casebolt, A. (2001). Subjugated knowledge in gender-integrated social work education: Call for dialogue. *Affilia, 16*, 411–431.

Fine, M. (1992). *Disruptive voices: The possibilities of feminist research*. Ann Arbor: University of Michigan Press.

Finn, J. L. (1994). The promise of participatory research. *Journal of Progressive Human Services, 5*(2), 25–42.

Fisher, R., Ury, W., & Patton, B. (1992). *Getting to yes: Negotiating agreement without giving in* (2nd ed.). Boston: Houghton Mifflin.

Fletcher, J. K. (1999a). *A radical perspective on power, gender and organizational change* (CGO Working Paper No. 5). Boston: Simmons Graduate School of Management, Center for Gender in Organizations.

Fletcher, J. K. (1999b). *Disappearing acts: Gender, power, and relational practice at work*. Boston: MIT Press.

Fletcher, J. K., & Jacques, R. (1999). *Relational practice: An emerging stream of theory and its significance for organizational studies* (CGO Working Paper No. 2). Boston: Simmons Graduate School of Management, Center for Gender in Organizations.

Flynn-Saulnier, C. (1996). *Feminist theories and social work: Approaches and applications*. New York: Haworth Press.

Fong, R. A., & Furuto, S. B. (Eds.). (2001). *Culturally-competent practice: Skills, interventions, and evaluations*. Needham Heights, MA: Allyn & Bacon.

Fortune, A. E., & Reid, W. J. (1999). *Research in social work* (3rd ed.). New York: Columbia University Press.

Foucault, M. (1980). *Power/knowledge: Selected interviews and other writings, 1972–1977*. New York: Pantheon Books.

Frankenberg, R. (1993). *White women, race matters: The social construction of whiteness*. Minneapolis: University of Minnesota Press.

Fraser, M. W. (1994). Scholarship and research in social work: Emerging challenges. *Journal of Social Work Education, 30*, 252–266.

Freedberg, S. (1993). The feminine ethic of care and the professionalization of social work. *Social Work, 38*, 535–540.

Freeman, S.J.M., Bourque, S. L., & Shelton, C. M. (Eds.). (2001). *Women on power: Leadership redefined*. Boston: Northeastern University Press.

Friere, P. (1973). *Education for critical consciousness*. New York: Seabury Press.

Friere, P. (1994). *Pedagogy of the oppressed*. New York: Continuum.

Furuto, S. M., Biswas, R., Chung, D. K., & Ross-Sheriff, F. (1992). *Social work practice with Asian Americans*. Newbury Park, CA: Sage Publications.

García-Gorena, V. (2001). Mothers as leaders: The madres Veracruzanas and the Mexican antinuclear movement. In S. J. Freeman, S. C. Bourque, & C. M. Shelton (Eds.), *Women on power: Leadership redefined* (pp. 236–264). Boston: Northeastern University Press.

Gardella, L. G. (1997). Prime mover: Pauline R. Lang. *Journal of Baccalaureate Social Work* 2(2), 22–42.

Gardella, L. G. (1999). Millie Charles: Believing in the mission. *Journal of Baccalaureate Social Work* 4(2), 19–35.

Garza, H. (1993). Second-class academics: Chicano/Latino faculty in U.S. universities. In J. Gainen & R. Boice (Eds.), *Building a diverse faculty* (pp. 33–41). San Francisco: Jossey-Bass.

Gaventa, J. (1993). The powerful, the powerless, and the experts: Knowledge struggles in an information age. In P. Park, M. Brydon-Miller, B. Hall, & T. Jackson (Eds.), *Voices of change: Participatory research in the United States and Canada* (pp. 21–40). Toronto: Ontario Institute for Studies in Education.

Germain, C. B., & Gitterman, A. (1996). *The life model of social work practice: Advances in theory and practice* (2nd ed.). New York: Columbia University Press.

Gibelman, M. (1999). Helping clients, helping ourselves: A social work agenda for achieving occupational equity. *Affilia, 14*, 400–416.

Gibelman, M. (2000). Say it ain't so, Norm! Reflections on who we are. *Social Work, 45*, 463–466.

Gibelman, M. (2003). *Navigating human services organizations: Essential information for thriving and surviving in agencies.* Chicago: Lyceum Books.

Gibson, M., & Ogbu, J. (1991). *Minority status and schooling: A comparative study of immigrant and involuntary minorities.* New York: Garland.

Gil, R. M., & Vazquez, C. I. (1996). *The Maria paradox: How Latinas can merge Old World traditions with New World self-esteem.* New York: Perigee.

Gilligan, C. (1982). *In a different voice: Psychological theory and women's development.* Cambridge, MA: Harvard University Press.

Gilligan, C., Lyons, N. P., & Hanmer, T. J. (1990). *Making connections: The relational worlds of adolescent girls at Emma Willard School.* Cambridge, MA: Harvard University Press.

Ginsberg, L., & Keys, P. R. (Eds.). (1995). *New management in human services* (2nd ed.). Washington, DC: NASW Press.

Gitterman, A., & Shulman, L. (1994). *Mutual aid groups, vulnerable populations, and the life cycle.* New York: Columbia University Press.

Glaser, B., & Strauss, A. (1967). *The discovering of grounded theory.* Chicago: Aldine.

Glater, J. D. (2001, March 26). Women are close to being majority of law students. *New York Times.* Retrieved from www.nytimes.com on April 1, 2001.

Glazer, M. P., & Glazer, P. M. (2001). Marching along with mothers and children. In S. J. Freeman, S. C. Bourque, & C. M. Shelton (Eds.), *Women on power: Leadership redefined* (pp. 199–235). Boston: Northeastern University Press.

Greenhaus, J. H., & Parasuraman, S. (2000). Research on work, family, and gender. In G. Powell (Ed.), *Handbook of gender and work* (pp. 391–412). Thousand Oaks, CA: Sage Publications.

Gross, E. (1999). Catching up with family change. *Affilia, 14*, 5–8.

Gutiérrez, L. M. (1990). Working with women of color: An empowerment perspective. *Social Work, 35*, 149–154.

Gutiérrez, L. M. (1992). Empowering clients in the twenty-first century: The role of human services organizations. In Y. Hasenfeld (Ed.), *Human service organizations as complex organizations* (pp. 320–328). Newbury Park, CA: Sage Publications.

Gutiérrez, L. M., GlenMaye, L., & DeLois, K. (1995). The organizational context of empowerment practice: Implications for social work administration. *Social Work, 40,* 249–258.

Gutiérrez, L. M., & Lewis, E. A. (Eds.). (1999). *Empowering women of color.* New York: Columbia University Press.

Gutiérrez, L. M., & Suarez, Z. (1999). Empowerment with Latinas. In L. M. Gutiérrez & E. A. Lewis (Eds.), *Empowering women of color* (pp. 167–186). New York: Columbia University Press.

Haney, C., & Hurtado, A. (1994). The jurisprudence of race and meritocracy: Standardized testing and "race-neutral" racism in the workplace. *Law and Human Behavior, 18*(3), 223–247.

Hanmer, J., & Statham, D. (1989). *Women and social work: Towards a woman-centered practice.* Chicago: Lyceum Books.

Harragan, B. L. (1977). *Games mother never taught you.* New York: Warner Books.

Hartling, L. M., & Ly, J. (2000). *Relational references: A selected bibliography of theory, research, and applications* (Stone Center Working Papers Series, Project Report No. 7). Wellesley, MA: Wellesley College, Stone Center.

Hartling, L. M., & Sparks, E. (2002). *Relational-cultural practice: Working in a nonrelational world* (Stone Center Working Papers Series, Work in Progress No. 97). Wellesley, MA: Wellesley College, Stone Center.

Hartman, A. (1992). In search of subjugated knowledge. *Social Work, 37,* 483–484.

Hartman, M. S. (Ed.). (1999). *Conversations with powerful women.* New Brunswick, NJ: Rutgers University Press.

Hartsock, N. (1990). Foucault on power: A theory for women? In L. J. Nicholson (Ed.), *Feminism/postmodernism* (pp. 157–175). New York: Routledge.

Havens, C., & Healy, L. (1991). Cabinet level appointees in Connecticut: Women making a difference. In D. Dodson (Ed.), *Gender and policymaking: Studies of women in office* (pp. 21–30). New Brunswick, NJ: Center for the Study of Women in Politics.

Haynes, K. S. (1989). *Women managers in human services.* New York: Springer.

Healy, L. M., Havens, C. M., & Chin, A. (1990). Preparing women for human service administration: Building on experience. *Administration in Social Work, 14*(2), 79–94.

Healy, L. M., Havens, C. M., & Pine, B. A. (1995). Women and social work management. In L. Ginsberg & P. R. Keys (Eds.), *New management in human services* (2nd ed., pp. 128–150). Washington, DC: NASW Press.

Heilbrun, C. G. (1988). *Writing a woman's life.* New York: Ballantine Books.

Helgeson, S. (1990). *The female advantage: Women's ways of leadership.* New York: Doubleday.

Henderson, N. R. (1995). A practical approach to analyzing and reporting focus groups studies: Lessons from qualitative market research. *Qualitative Health Research,* 5, 463–578.

Henning, M., & Jardim, A. (1977). *The managerial woman.* Garden City, New York: Anchor.

Herr, K. (1995). Action research as empowering practice. *Journal of Progressive Human Services,* 6(2), 45–58.

Hertz, R. (Ed.). (1997). *Reflexivity and voice.* Thousand Oaks, CA: Sage Publications.

Heskin, A. D. (1991). *The struggle for community.* Boulder, CO: Westview Press.

Hesselbein, F. (1999). Managing a world that is round. In F. Hesselbein & P. M. Cohen (Eds.), *Leader to leader: Enduring insights on leadership from the Drucker Foundation's award-winning journal* (pp. 9–14). San Francisco: Jossey-Bass.

Hewlett, S. A. (2002). *Creating a life: Professional women and the quest for children.* New York: Talk Miramax Books.

Higginbotham, E., & Weber, L. (Eds.). (1992). Moving up with kin and community: Upward social mobility for black and white women. *Gender and Society,* 6, 416–440.

Higginbotham, E., & Weber, L. (1999). Perceptions of workplace discrimination among black and white professional-managerial women. In I. Browne (Ed.), *Latinas and African American women at work: Race, gender, and ethnicity* (pp. 327–356). New York: Russell Sage Foundation.

Hochschild, A. R. (1989). *The second shift.* New York: Avon Books.

Hochschild, A. R. (1997). *The time bind: When work becomes home and home becomes work.* New York: Henry Holt.

Hodges, V. G. (2001). Historical development of African American child welfare services. In I. B. Carlton-LaNey (Ed.), *African American leadership: An empowerment tradition in social welfare history* (pp. 203–214). Washington, DC: NASW Press.

Holbrook, T. L. (1995). Finding subjugated knowledge: Personal document research. *Social Work, 40,* 746–752.

Hollands, J. A. (2001). *Same game, different rules: How to get ahead without being a bully broad, ice queen, or other "Ms. Understood."* New York: McGraw-Hill.

Holvino, E. (2001). *Complicating gender: The simultaneity of race, gender, and class in organizational change(ing)* (CGO Working Paper No. 14). Boston: Simmons Graduate School of Management, Center for Gender in Organizations.

hooks, b. (1984). *Feminist theory: From the margin to center.* Boston: South End Press.

hooks, b. (1989). *Talking back: Thinking feminist, thinking black.* Boston: South End Press.

hooks, b. (1994). *Outlaw culture: Resisting representatives.* New York: Routledge.

hooks, b. (2000). *Where we stand: Class matters.* New York: Routledge.

Hooyman, N. R., & Cunningham, R. (1986). An alternative administrative style. In N. Van Den Bergh & L. B. Cooper (Eds.), *Feminist visions for social work* (pp. 163–186). Silver Spring, MD: National Association of Social Workers.

Hopkins, N. (1999, July 20). Testimony, CAWMSET (Commission on the Advancement of Women and Minorities in Science, Engineering, and Technology and Development) Public Hearing. Retrieved from www.nsf.gov/od/cswmset/meetings/hearing-990720/nhopkins/nhopkins.htm on August 30, 2003.

Hopps, J. G., & Pinderhughes, E. (1999). *Groupwork with overwhelmed clients.* New York: Free Press.

Hurtado, A. (1989). Relating to privilege: Seduction and rejections in the subordination of white women and women of color. *Signs: Journal of Women in Culture and Society, 14,* 833–855.

Hurtado, A. (1999). *Disappearing dynamics of women of color* (CGO Working Paper No. 4). Boston: Simmons Graduate School of Management, Center for Gender in Organizations.

Iannello, K. P. (1992). *Decisions without hierarchy: Feminist interventions in organization theory and practice.* New York: Routledge.

Iglehart, A. P., & Becerra, R. M. (2000). *Social services and the ethnic community.* Prospect Heights, IL: Waveland Press.

Institute for Higher Education Policy. (2001). *Getting through college: Voices of low-income and minority students in New England.* Braintree, MA: Nellie Mae Foundation.

International Federation of Social Workers. (2002). *Draft document: Ethics in social work, statement of principles*. Geneva: Author. Retrieved from www.ifsw.org on May 1, 2003.

Jacobson, J. (2001, June 8). Study documents lack of diversity in chemistry departments. *Chronicle of Higher Education*. Retrieved from www.chronicle.org on June 12, 2001.

Jaeger, C. C., Schule, R., & Kasemir, B. (1999). Focus groups in integrated assessment: A micro-cosmos for reflexive modernization. *Innovation: The European Journal of Social Sciences, 12*(2), 195–220.

Jamieson, K. H. (1995). *Beyond the double bind: Women and leadership*. New York: Oxford University Press.

Jarrold, J. S., & Lazzari, M. M. (2001). The relational model of identity development: An essential curricular component for social work education and practice. *Journal of Baccalaureate Social Work, 7*(1), 95–110.

Jennings, J., Martin, R. R., & Vroom, P. I. (1998). African American women in academic leadership. In A. Daly (Ed.), *Workplace diversity: Issues and perspectives* (pp. 166–175). Washington, DC: NASW Press.

Jones, J. (1985). *Labor of love, labor of sorrow: Black women, work and the family, from slavery to the present*. New York: Random House.

Jordan, J. V. (Ed.). (1997). *Women's growth in diversity: More writings from the Stone Center*. New York: Guilford Press.

Jordan, J. V. (1999). *Toward connection and competence* (Stone Center Working Paper Series, Work in Progress No. 83). Wellesley, MA: Wellesley College, Stone Center.

Jordan, J. V., Kaplan, A. G., Miller, J. B., Stiver, I. P., & Surrey, J. L. (Eds.). (1991). *Women's growth in connection: Writings from the Stone Center*. New York: Guilford Press.

Joyner, M. C. (2001). Reflections of leadership. *Journal of Baccalaureate Social Work, 6*(2), 1–7.

Kelly, M. J., & Post, K. A. (1995). Mentoring and networking in human services. In L. Ginsberg & P. R. Keys (Eds.), *New management in human services* (2nd ed., pp. 151–161). Washington, DC: NASW Press.

Kidd, P. S., & Parshall, M. B. (2000). Getting the focus and the group: Enhancing analytical rigor in focus group research. *Qualitative Health Research, 10*, 293–309.

Kivel, B. D., & Wells, J. W. (1998). Working it out: What managers should know about gay men, lesbians, and bisexual people and their employment issues. In A. Daly (Ed.), *Workplace diversity: Issues and perspectives* (pp. 103–115). Washington, DC: NASW Press.

Kolb, D. M., Fletcher, J., Meyerson, D., Merrill-Sands, D., & Ely, R. (1998). *Making change: A framework for promoting gender equity in organizations* (CGO Insights No. 1). Boston: Simmons Graduate School of Management, Center for Gender in Organizations.

Kolb, D. M., & Merrill-Sands, D. (1999). *Waiting for outcomes: Anchoring gender equity and organizational changes in cultural assumptions* (CGO Working Paper No. 1). Boston: Simmons Graduate School of Management, Center for Gender in Organizations.

Kolb, D. M., & Williams, J. (2000). *The shadow negotiation: How women can master the hidden agendas that determine bargaining success.* New York: Simon & Schuster.

Krueger, R. A., & King, J. A. (1998). Involving community members in focus groups. In *The focus group kit.* Thousand Oaks, CA: Sage Publications.

Lackland, S.D. (2000). Psychological adaptation of adolescents with immigrant backgrounds. *Journal of Social Psychology, 140*(1), 5–26.

Lambert, S. J., & Hopkins, K. (1995). Occupational conditions and workers' sense of community: Variations by gender and race. *American Journal of Community Psychology, 23*(2), 151–179.

Lather, P. (1991). *Getting smart: Feminist research and pedagogy with/in the postmodern.* New York: Routledge.

The Latina Feminist Group. (2001). *Telling to live: Latina feminist testimonios.* Durham, NC: Duke University Press.

Lee, J.A.B. (2001). *The empowerment approach to social work practice: Building the beloved community* (2nd ed.). New York: Columbia University Press.

Leighninger, L. (1987). *Social work: Search for identity.* Westport, CT: Greenwood Press.

Lewin, K. (1948/1940). *Resolving social conflicts: Selected papers on group dynamics.* New York: Harper & Row.

Lewin, T. (2001, May 13). Taking care: It's not just for mothers anymore. *New York Times Week in Review.* Retrieved from www.nytimes.com on May 14, 2001.

Lewis, E. (1999). Staying the path: Lessons about health and resistance from women of the African Diaspora in the United States. In L. M. Gutiérrez & E. Lewis (Eds.), *Empowering women of color* (pp. 150–167). New York: Columbia University Press.

Loden, M. (1985). *Feminine leadership.* New York: Times Books.

Loden, M. (1995). *Implementing diversity.* New York: McGraw-Hill.

Longres, J. F. (2000). *Human behavior in the social environment* (3rd ed.). Itasca, IL: F. E. Peacock Publishers.

Longres, J. F., & Scanlon, E. (2001). Social justice and the research curriculum. *Journal of Social Work Education, 37*, 447–464.

López, R. A. (1999). *Las comadres* as a social support system. *Affilia, 14*, 24–41.

Lorde, A. (1981). An open letter to Mary Daly. In C. Moraga & G. Anzaldúa (Eds.), *A bridge called my back: Writings of radical women of color* (pp. 94–97). New York: Kitchen Table Press.

Lorde, A. (1984). *Sister outsider*. Trumansburg, NY: Crossing Press.

Lum, D. (1999). *Culturally competent practice: A framework for growth and action*. New York: Brooks/Cole.

Lynch, D., Vernon, R., & Folaron, G. (2001, November 2). *Integrating technology in the curriculum: Research and the Internet*. Paper presented at the 19th annual conference of the Association of Baccalaureate Social Work Program Directors, Denver.

MacDougall, C., & Baum, F. (1997). The devil's advocate: A strategy to avoid groupthink and stimulate discussion in focus groups. *Qualitative Health Research, 7*, 532–541.

Maguire, P. (1987). *Doing participatory research: A feminist approach*. Amherst, MA: Center for International Education.

Malson, M., Mudimbe-Boyi, E., O'Barr, J., & Wyer, M. (1988). *Black women in America*. Chicago: University of Chicago Press.

Marks, R., Hassim, S., January-Bardill, N., Khumalo, B., & Olckers, I. (2000). *Gender, race, and class dynamics in post-apartheid South Africa* (CGO Working Paper No. 9). Boston: Simmons Graduate School of Management, Center for Gender in Organizations.

Martin, R. R. (1995). *Oral history in social work: Research, assessment, and intervention*. Thousand Oaks, CA: Sage Publications.

Mayo-Quiñones, Y., & Resnick, R. P. (1996). The impact of machismo on Hispanic women. *Affilia, 11*, 257–277.

McIntosh, P. (1995). White privilege and male privilege: A personal account to coming to see correspondence through work in women's studies. In M. S. Andersen & P. H. Collins (Eds.), *Race, class and gender: An anthology* (2nd ed., pp. 70–81). Belmont, CA: Wadsworth.

Medina, C., & Luna, G. (2000). Narratives from Latina professors in higher education. *Anthropology and Education Quarterly, 31*(1), 47–66.

Meier, M. H. (2001, November 1). Leaders say managing kids prepared them to be boss. *Women's Enews*. Retrieved from www.womensenews.org on November 3, 2001.

Mergal, M. (1993). Puerto Rican feminism at a crossroad: Challenges at the turn of the century. In E. Meléndez & E. Meléndez (Eds.), *Colonial dilemma: Critical perspectives of contemporary Puerto Rico* (pp. 131–142). Boston: South End Press.

Merrill-Sands, D., Fletcher, J. K., Acosta, A., Starks, A. S., Andrews, N., & Harvey, M. (1999). *Engendering organizational change: A case study of strengthening gender equity and organizational effectiveness through transforming work culture and practices* (CGO Working Paper No. 3). Boston: Simmons Graduate School of Management, Center for Gender in Organizations.

Merrill-Sands, D., & Kolb, D. M. (2001, April). *Women as leaders: The paradox of success* (CGO Insights No. 9). Boston: Simmons Graduate School of Management, Center for Gender in Organizations.

Meyerson, D. E. (2001). *Tempered radicals: How people use difference to inspire change at work*. Cambridge, MA: Harvard Business School Press.

Meyerson, D. E., & Fletcher, J. K. (2000). A modest manifesto for shattering the glass ceiling. *Harvard Business Review, 78*(1), 126–136.

Meyerson, D. E., & Scully, M. (1999). *Tempered radicalism: Changing the workplace from within* (CGO Insights No. 6). Boston: Simmons Graduate School of Management, Center for Gender in Organizations.

Miller, J. B. (1976). *Toward a new psychology of women*. Boston: Beacon Press.

Miller, J. B. (1991a). The development of women's sense of self. In J. V. Jordan, A. G. Kaplan, J. B. Miller, I. P. Stiver, & J. L. Surrey (Eds.), *Women's growth in connection: Writings from the Stone Center* (pp. 11–26). New York: Guilford Press.

Miller, J. B. (1991b). Women and power. In J. V. Jordan, A. G. Kaplan, J. B. Miller, I. P. Stiver, & J. L. Surrey (Eds.), *Women's growth in connection: Writings from the Stone Center* (pp. 197–205). New York: Guilford Press.

Miller, J. B., & Stiver, I. P. (1997). *The healing connection: How women form relationships in therapy and in life*. Boston: Beacon Press.

Min, P. G., & Kim, R. (1999). *Struggle for ethnic identity: Narratives by Asian American professionals*. Walnut Creek, CA: AltaMira Press.

Mindell, P. A. (1995). *A woman's guide to the language of success: Communication with confidence and power*. Englewood Cliffs, NJ: Prentice Hall.

Mizrahi, T., & Rosenthal, B. B. (2001). Complexities of coalition building: Leaders' successes, strategies, struggles, and solutions. *Social Work, 46,* 63–78.

Moen, P. (1992). *Women's two roles: A contemporary dilemma.* New York: Auburn House.

Molloy, J. (1977). *The women's dress for success book.* New York: Warner Books.

Morgan, D. L. (1998). Planning focus groups. In *The focus group kit.* Thousand Oaks, CA: Sage Publications.

Morrison, T. (Ed.). (1992). *Race-ing justice, En-gendering power: Essays on Anita Hill, Clarence Thomas, and the construction of social reality.* New York: Pantheon Books.

Murrell, A. J., Crosby, F. J., & Ely, R. J. (Eds.). (1999). *Mentoring dilemmas: Developmental relationships within multicultural organizations.* Hillsdale, NJ: Lawrence Erlbaum.

Nagel, J. (1994). Constructing ethnicity: Creating and re-creating ethnic identity and culture. *Social Problems, 41*(1), 152–176.

Naples, N. A. (1997). *Grassroots warriors: Activist mothering, community work, and the war on poverty.* New York: Routledge.

National Association of Social Workers. (1999). *NASW code of ethics.* Washington, DC: Author.

National Association of Social Workers. (2001). *NASW standards for cultural competence in social work practice.* Washington, DC: Author.

National Education Association. (1991). Minority mentoring. In *Almanac of higher education* (pp. 156–160). Washington, DC: Author.

Nieves-Squires, S. (1991). *Latina women: Making their presence on campus less tenuous.* Washington, DC: Association of American Colleges.

Nkomo, S. M. (1996). Identities and the complexity of diversity. In S. E. Jackson & M. N. Ruderman (Eds.), *Diversity in work teams: Research paradigms for a changing workplace* (pp. 247–254). Washington, DC: American Psychological Association.

Noddings, N. (1984). *Caring: A feminine approach to ethics and moral education.* Berkeley: University of California Press.

O'Neill, J. V. (2001, January 1). Network reports membership data. *NASW News, 46*(1), pp. 1, 8.

Ortíz, A. (Ed.). (1996). *Puerto Rican women and work: Bridges in transnational labor.* Philadelphia: Temple University Press.

Ortíz, V. (1996). Migration and marriage among Puerto Rican women. *International Migration Review, 30*(2), 460–481.

Padilla, R. V., & Chavez, R. C. (Eds.). (1995). *The leaning ivory tower: Latino professors in American universities.* Albany: State University of New York Press.

Pantoja, A. (2002). *Memoir of a visionary: Antonia Pantoja.* Houston: Arte Público Press.

Parks, S. D. (2000). *Big questions, worthy dreams: Mentoring young adults in their search for meaning, purpose, and faith.* San Francisco: Jossey-Bass.

Pennell, J., & Ristock, J. L. (1999). Feminist links, postmodern interruptions: Critical pedagogy and social work. *Affilia, 14,* 460–481.

Phelan, S. (1993). (Be)coming out: Lesbian identity and politics. *Signs, 18,* 765–790.

Pinderhughes, E. (1989). *Understanding race, ethnicity, and power: The key to efficacy in clinical practice.* New York: Free Press.

Poster, W. R. (1995). The challenges and promises of class and racial diversity in the women's movement: A study of two women's organizations. *Gender and Society, 9,* 659–679.

Powell, G. N. (Ed.). (1990). One more time: Do female and male managers differ? *Academy of Management Executives, 4,* 68–74.

Prashad, V. (2000). *The karma of brown folk.* Minneapolis: University of Minnesota.

President's Advisory Commission on Educational Excellence for Latina Americans. (1996). *Our nation on the fault line: Latina American education.* Washington, DC: Author.

Purkayastha, B., Raman, S., & Bhide, K. (1997). Empowering women: SNEHA's multifaceted activism. In S. Shah (Ed.), *Dragon ladies: Asian American feminists breathe fire* (pp. 100–107). Boston: South End Press.

Raggins, B. R. (1999). Gender and mentoring relationships: A review and research agenda for the next decade. In G. N. Powell (Ed.), *Mentoring dilemmas: Developmental relationships within multicultural organizations.* Hillsdale, NJ: Lawrence Erlbaum.

Raman, S. (1999, November 16). *Being situated on multiple margins.* Paper presented at Amba: South Asian Women Negotiating/Contesting Multiple Boundaries, University of Connecticut, West Hartford, CT.

Ramos, J. (1994). *Compañeras: Latina lesbians.* New York: Routledge.

Rank, M. G., & Hutchison, W. S. (2000). An analysis of leadership within the social work profession. *Journal of Social Work Education, 36,* 487–502.

Rao, A., Rieky, S., & Kelleher, D. (1999). *Gender at work: Organizational change for equity.* West Hartford, CT: Kumarian Press.

Reese, D. J., Ahern, R. E., Nair, S., O'Faire, J. D., & Warren, C. (1999). Hospice access and use by African Americans: Addressing cultural and institutional barriers through participatory action research. *Social Work, 44,* 549–559.

Reid-Merritt, P. (1996). *Sister power: How phenomenal black women are rising to the top.* New York: John Wiley & Sons.

Reinharz, S. (1992). *Feminist methods in social research.* New York: Oxford University Press.

Reskin, B. F. (1998). *The realities of affirmative action in employment.* Washington, DC: American Sociological Association.

Reskin, B. F. (1999). Occupational segregation by race and ethnicity among women workers. In I. Browne (Ed.), *Latinas and African American women at work: Race, gender, and economic inequality* (pp. 183–206). New York: Russell Sage Foundation.

Ristock, J. L., & Pennell, J. (1996). *Community research as empowerment: Feminist links, postmodern interruptions.* New York: Oxford University Press.

Romero, M. (1997). Epilogue. In E. Higginbotham & M. Romero (Eds.), *Women and work: Exploring race, ethnicity, and class* (pp. 235–248). Thousand Oaks, CA: Sage Publications.

Rosener, J. B. (1995). *America's competitive secret: Women managers.* New York: Oxford University Press.

Rothenberg, P. (2000). *Invisible privilege: A memoir about race, class, and gender.* Lawrence: University of Kansas Press.

Rothenberg, P. (Ed.). (2001). *White privilege: Essential readings on the other side of racism.* Lawrence: University of Kansas Press.

Rubin, A., & Babbie, E. (1993). *Research methods for social work.* Pacific Grove, CA: Brooks/Cole.

Ruderman, M. N., & Ohlott, P. J. (2002). *Standing at the crossroads: Next steps for high-achieving women.* San Francisco: Jossey-Bass.

Sam, D. L. (2000). Psychological adaptation of adolescents with immigrant backgrounds. *Journal of Social Psychology, 140*(1), 5–26.

Schriver, J. M. (1995). As we begin: Collaboration, listening and diverse research methods. *Journal of Baccalaureate Social Work, 1*(1), 9–11.

Scott, J. W. (1988). *Gender and the politics of history.* New York: Columbia University Press.

Scott, K. (1991). *The habit of surviving: Black women's strategies for life.* New Brunswick, NJ: Rutgers University Press.

Segura, D. A. (1994). Inside the work worlds of Chicana and Mexican immigrant women. In M. B. Zinn & B. T. Dill (Eds.), *Women of color in U.S. society* (pp. 203–227). Philadelphia: Temple University Press.

Shah, S. (Ed.). (1997). *Dragon ladies: Asian American feminists breathe fire*. Boston: South End Press.

Shaw, S. J. (1996). *What a woman ought to be and do: Black professional women workers during the Jim Crow era*. Chicago: University of Chicago Press.

Smith, M. W. (1995). Ethics in focus groups: A few concerns. *Qualitative Health Research, 5*, 478–487.

SNEHA, Inc. (n.d.). [Brochure]. Cheshire, CT: Author.

Solomon, B. (1976). *Black empowerment*. New York: Columbia University Press.

Solomon, B. (1987). Empowerment: Social work in oppressed communities. *Journal of Social Work Practice, 2*(4), 79–91.

Spencer, R. (2000). *A comparison of relational psychologies* (Stone Center Working Papers Series, Project Report No. 5). Wellesley, MA: Wellesley College, Stone Center.

Sprang, G., Secret, M., & Bradford, J. (1999). Blending work and family: A case study. *Affilia, 14*, 98–116.

Stoller, E. P., & Gibson, R. C. (Eds.). (2000). *Worlds of difference: Inequality in the aging experience* (3rd ed.). Thousand Oaks, CA: Pine Forge.

Stoutland, S. E. (1997). *Neither urban jungle nor urban village: Women, families, and community development*. New York: Garland.

Strauss, A., & Corbin, J. (1994). Grounded theory methodology: An overview. In N. K. Denzin & Y. S. Lincoln (Eds.), *Handbook of qualitative research* (pp. 273–285). Thousand Oaks, CA: Sage Publications.

Strauss, A., & Corbin, J. (1997). *Grounded theory in practice*. Newbury Park, CA: Sage Publications.

A study on the status of women faculty in science at MIT (1999, March). *MIT Faculty Newsletter, 11*(4). Retrieved from web.mit.edu/fnl/women/women/html on August 31, 2003.

Sue, D. W., Carter, R. T., Cases, J. M., & Fouad, N. A. (1998). *Multicultural counseling competencies: Individual and organizational development*. Thousand Oaks, CA: Sage Publications.

Swigonski, M. E. (1994). The logic of feminist standpoint theory for social work research. *Social Work, 39*, 387–392.

Swiss, D. J. (1996). *Women breaking through: Overcoming the final ten obstacles at work*. Princeton, NJ: Peterson's Pacesetter Books.

Tannen, D. (1990). *You just don't understand*. New York: Wm. Morrow.

Tannen, D. (1996). *Talking from 9 to 5: Women and men in the workplace: Language, sex and power*. New York: Wm. Morrow.

Thomas, D. A. (1989). Mentoring and irrationality: The role of racial taboos. *Human Resource Management, 28*(2), 279–290.

Thomas, D. A. (1998). Mentoring and diversity in organizations: Importance of race and gender in work relationships. In A. Daly (Ed.), *Workplace diversity: Issues and perspectives* (pp. 281–292). Washington, DC: NASW Press.

Thomas, D. A. (2001). The truth about mentoring minorities: Race matters. *Harvard Business Review, 79*(4), 98–107.

Thomas, D. A., & Gabarro, J. J. (1999). *Breaking through: The making of minority executives in corporate America*. Boston: Harvard Business School Press.

Thomas, K. M., Phillips, L. D., & Brown, S. (1998). Redefining race in the workplace: Insights from ethnic identity theory. *Journal of Black Psychology, 24*(1), 76–92.

Thomas, R. R., Jr. (1996). *Redefining diversity*. New York: AMACOM, American Management Association.

Tierney, W. G., & Bensimon, E. M. (1996). *Promotion and tenure: Community and socialization in academe*. Albany: State University of New York Press.

Tobitt, J. E. (1946). *The ditty bag*. New York, Girl Scouts USA.

Torruellas, R. M., Benmayor, R., & Juarbe, A. (1996). Negotiating gender, work and welfare: Familia as a productive labor among Puerto Rican women in New York City. In A. Ortíz (Ed.), *Puerto Rican women and work: Bridges in transnational labor*. Philadelphia: Temple University Press.

Triandis, H. C. (1996). The importance of contexts in studies of diversity. In S. E. Jackson & M. N. Ruderman (Eds.), *Diversity in work teams: Research paradigms for a changing workplace* (pp. 225–234). Washington, DC: American Psychological Association.

Trujillo, C. (Ed.). (1991). *Chicana lesbians: The girls our mothers warned us about*. Berkeley, CA: Third Women Press.

Turner, C. (1991). Feminist practice with women of color: A developmental perspective. In M. Bricker-Jenkins, N. R. Hooyman, & N.

Gottlieb (Eds.), *Feminist social work practice in clinical settings* (pp. 108–127). Newbury Park, CA: Sage Publications.

University of Houston–Victoria. (2001). Letting Education Achieve Dreams (LEAD) Initiative: Summary. Victoria, TX: Author.

U.S. Department of Labor, Bureau of Labor Statistics. (1998). *Tabulations from the current population survey, 1998 annual averages.* Washington, DC: Author.

Van Den Bergh, N. (Ed.). (1995). *Feminist practice in the 21st century.* Washington, DC: NASW Press.

Van Den Bergh, N. (1998). Managing biculturalism at the workplace: A group approach. In A. Daly (Ed.), *Workplace diversity: Issues and perspectives* (pp. 243–252). Washington, DC: NASW Press.

Van Den Bergh, N., & Cooper, L. B. (1986). Introduction. In N. Van Den Bergh & L. B. Cooper (Eds.), *Feminist visions for social work* (pp. 1–28). Silver Spring, MD: National Association of Social Workers.

Van Hook, M., Hugen, B., & Aguilar, M. (Eds.). (2002). *Spirituality within religious traditions in social work practice.* Pacific Grove, CA: Brooks/Cole.

Vansina, J. (1985). *Oral tradition as history.* Madison: University of Wisconsin.

Vasquez, M.J.T. (1997). Confronting barriers to the participation of Mexican American women in higher education. In A. Darder, T. Rodolfo, & H. Gutiérrez (Eds.), *Latinos in higher education* (pp. 454–467). New York: Routledge.

Vaz, K. M. (1995). *Black women in America.* Newbury Park, CA: Sage Publications.

Vaz, K. M. (Ed.). (1997a). *Oral narrative research with black women.* Thousand Oaks, CA: Sage Publications.

Vaz, K. M. (1997b). Social conformity and social resistance: Women's perspectives on "women's place." In K. M. Vaz (Ed.), *Oral narrative research with black women* (pp. 223–249). Thousand Oaks, CA: Sage Publications.

Vernon, R., Lynch, D., & Folaron, G. (2000, February 26–29). *Using the Web for research.* Paper presented at the annual program meeting of the Council on Social Work Education, New York.

Walker, M. (2002). *Power and effectiveness: Envisioning an alternative paradigm* (Stone Center Working Paper Series, Work in Progress No. 94). Wellesley, MA: Wellesley College, Stone Center.

Wayne, R. (2002, May 17). *Focus groups: A participatory research method for the social work practitioner.* Paper presented at the annual conference of the National Association of Social Workers, Farmington, CT.

Weaver, H. N. (2000). Culture and professional education: The experiences of Native American social workers. *Journal of Social Work Education, 36,* 415–428.

Weick, A. (2000). Hidden voices. *Social Work, 45,* 395–402.

Weick, K. (1984). Small wins: Redefining the scale of social problems. *American Psychologist, 39,* 40–49.

Weil, M. (1986). Women, community, and organizing. In N. Van Den Bergh & L. B. Cooper (Eds.), *Feminist visions for social work* (pp. 1–28). Silver Spring, MD: National Association of Social Workers.

Wellington, S., & Catalyst. (2001). *Be your own mentor: Strategies from top women on the secrets of success.* New York: Random House.

Wenger, E. C., & Snyder, W. M. (2000). Communities of practice: The organizational frontier. *Harvard Business Review, 78*(1), 139–145.

Wheatley, M. J. (1999). *Leadership and the new science: Discovering order in a chaotic world.* San Francisco: Berrett-Koehler.

White, J. Z. (1998). Supervision and management of American Indian social and human services workers. In A. Daly (Ed.), *Workplace diversity: Issues and perspectives* (pp. 36–44). Washington, DC: NASW Press.

Whyte, W. G. (1991). *Participatory action research.* Newbury Park, CA: Sage Publications.

Williams, J. (2000). *Unbending gender: Why family and work conflict and what to do about it.* New York: Oxford University Press.

Wilson, P. P., Valentine, D., & Pereira, A. (2002). Perceptions of new social work faculty about mentoring experiences. *Journal of Social Work Education, 38,* 317–334.

Witkin, S. L. (2000). Writing social work. *Social Work, 45,* 389–394.

Women in Development of Greater Boston. (1992). *Getting what you deserve: A reference guide to compensation and salary negotiation.* Boston: Author.

Woo, D. (2000). *Glass ceilings and Asian Americans: The new face of workplace barriers.* Walnut Creek, CA: AltaMira Press.

Wright, R., Jr., Euster, G., Gardella, L. G., Pollard, W., & Shulman, L. (2000). Scholarship revisited: An examination of faculty work in social work education. In R. Diamond & A. Bronwyn (Eds.), *The disciplines speak II: More statements on rewarding the scholarly, professional, and creative work of faculty* (pp. 201–224). Syracuse, NY: Syracuse University.

Wu, D.T.L. (1997). *Asian Pacific Americans in the workplace.* Walnut Creek, CA: AltaMira Press.

Young, D. S., & Wright, E. M. (2001). Mothers making tenure. *Journal of Social Work Education, 37,* 555–570.

Zedeck, S. (Ed.). (1992). *Work, families and organizations.* San Francisco: Jossey-Bass.

Zweigenhaft, R. L., & Domhoff, G. W. (1998). *Diversity in the power elite.* New Haven, CT: Yale University Press.

About the Authors

Lorrie Greenhouse Gardella, JD, MSW, ACSW, is professor and chair of the Department of Social Work at Saint Joseph College in West Hartford, Connecticut. She began her social work career at West Haven Community House, and she worked as a consultant in children's law to the Connecticut State Department of Children and Youth Services. A national leader in social work education, she has served as president of the Association of Baccalaureate Social Work Program Directors and on the boards of directors of the Council on Social Work Education, the Institute for the Advancement of Social Work Research, and on the editorial board of the *Journal of Baccalaureate Social Work*. She chaired the board of trustees of the National Association of Social Workers Legal Defense Fund. She has published in the areas of child welfare, social work history, and social work with communities and groups.

Karen S. Haynes, PhD, MSW, is president of California State University–San Marcos. She previously served as president of the University of Houston–Victoria and as dean of the University of Houston Graduate School of Social Work. She is secretary-treasurer of the board of the American Association of State Colleges and Universities. She has published articles on political social work and three other books: *Women Managers in Human Services*; *Affecting Change: Social Workers in the Political Arena* with Jim Mickelson; and *Invitation to Social Work* with Karen Holmes. She recently completed a book chapter titled "Women's Issues: An Intergenerational Perspective" with her daughter, Kimberly Haynes, a social worker.

MORE RESOURCES FROM NASW PRESS

A Dream and a Plan: *A Woman's Path to Leadership in Human Services,* by Lorrie Greenhouse Gardella and Karen S. Haynes. The helping professions are rich with women who have the imagination and aspiration to be successful leaders, but lack confidence or opportunity. Written from an inclusive, multicultural perspective, this empowering book offers practical guidance on pursuing career advancement, overcoming barriers, and cultivating mentorship. A pragmatic and motivating text for social workers, students, and human services providers, as well as for experienced managers.

ISBN: 0-87101-359-2. 2004. Item #3592. $35.99.

Changing Hats while Managing Change: *From Social Work Practice to Administration, 2nd Edition,* by Felice Davidson Perlmutter and Wendy P. Crook. A unique and useful guide for practitioners who want to broaden their repertoire of professional choices and are either moving up the administrative ladder or considering making a career move in that direction. In user-friendly language, *Changing Hats* addresses the major challenges that face social workers in these complex times and presents a picture of the various roles and responsibilities of administration, illustrating them with lively case studies.

ISBN: 0-87101-361-4. 2004. Item #3614. $44.99.

Interactional Supervision, *by Lawrence Shulman. Interactional Supervision* offers practical strategies for formal and informal supervision and helps human services supervisors develop skills for working with staff individually and in groups. Shulman's real-life strategies identify and explain management skills needed in every phase of supervisory work. Based on his extensive research, Shulman presents solutions to problems that supervisors face on a day-to-day basis.

ISBN: 0-87101-220-0. 1992. Item #2200. $43.99.

New Management in Human Services, *2nd Edition,* Leon Ginsberg and Paul R. Keys, *Editors.* An invaluable guidebook on working with boards, boosting staff morale, and improving service delivery, *New Management in Human Services* should be on every manager's bookshelf. The editors use case examples to illustrate management practices and offer important information on fiscal accountability, team building, working with the media, member services, and organizational viability in a competitive era.

ISBN: 0-87101-251-0. 1995. Item #2510. $34.99.

(Order form and information on reverse side)

ORDER FORM

Qty.	Title	Item #	Price	Total
__	A Dream and a Plan	3592	$35.99	_____
__	Changing Hats while Managing Change	3614	$44.99	_____
__	Interactional Supervision	2200	$43.99	_____
__	New Management in Human Services	2510	$34.99	_____

Subtotal	_____
Postage and Handling	_____
DC residents add 6% sales tax	_____
MD residents add 5% sales tax	_____
NC residents add 4.5% sales tax	_____
NJ residents add 6% sales tax	_____
Total	_____

POSTAGE AND HANDLING
Minimum postage and handling fee is $4.95. Orders that do not include appropriate postage and handling will be returned.

DOMESTIC: Please add 12% to orders under $100 for postage and handling. For orders over $100 add 7% of order.

CANADA: Please add 17% postage and handling.

OTHER INTERNATIONAL: Please add 22% postage and handling.

❏ **Check or money order** (payable to NASW Press) for $ _____.

❏ **Credit card**
   ❏ Visa   ❏ MasterCard   ❏ American Express

_____   _____

Credit Card Number   Expiration Date

Signature _____

Name _____

Address _____

City _____ State/Province _____

Country _____ Zip _____

Phone _____ E-mail _____

NASW Member # (if applicable) _____

(Please make checks payable to NASW Press. Prices are subject to change.)

NASW PRESS
P. O. Box 431
Annapolis JCT, MD 20701
USA

Credit card orders call
1-800-227-3590
(In the Metro Wash., DC, area, call 301-317-8688)
Or fax your order to 301-206-7989
Or order online at www.naswpress.org

CPDP06